THE JOY CITY POOL

SMOKE & MIRRORS

GLENN BRIGGS

Edited by Michelle Krueger

Cover design by Haze Long

ISBN: 978-1-7369323-4-6 (paperback)
978-1-7369323-5-3 (hardback)

This book is dedicated to my mother and father,
Vikitha M Briggs and Glenn L Briggs,
and my Godmother, Barbara J Anderson.

Other books of the series:

THE JOY CITY POOL

THE JOY CITY POOL
CHASING GHOSTS

TABLE OF CONTENTS

THE JOY CITY POOL

SMOKE & MiRRORS

Chapter 1

Poached

There were just four days until the happiest day of the year, or so what most people believed that day to be. Christmas, the day parents were able to finally let out a sigh of relief as their children let out cheers of joy.

Even as nasty and wretched of a place as Joy City was, holiday spirit did still exist inside of it. Whether simply smiling a little more than usual, speaking to someone they normally wouldn't have, or performing even the smallest random act of kindness towards a stranger, Christmastime changed those within Joy City a bit into what resembled happy people.

In the areas of the city that weren't completely run down, every so often a crowd of carolers would walk door to door attempting to spread holiday joy through song. Families would line up inside the local mall for a free picture with Santa Claus in between their shopping. The entire aura of the city was different during the final month of the year. People seemed happier, more sociable, more willing to lend a helping hand even. It was as if everyone in the city had been infected by some sort of Christmas bug that changed the way they moved about day to day.

However, while most changed there were a few who didn't, a few to whom Christmas was nothing more than another day that would pass in twenty-four hours, and so they lived it the same as any other day. They got up in the morning, did whatever job they needed to do, fulfilled whatever responsibilities they were expected to, and laid down to sleep at night just the same as they would any other day.

"Hors d'oeuvres ma'am?" a man in a tuxedo vest asked. He was holding a small tray of finger foods.

Kim turned around to face him and smiled, "Oh, no thank you."

The man nodded with a smile and walked away asking the same of the next closest person.

Kim turned around to a table covered in a red cloth, garnished in artificial mistletoe and holiday themed lights. She grabbed a glass and used a ladle to scoop herself some punch from the large bowl resting on the table. She turned back around and took slow sips as she scanned her surroundings.

She was at a Christmas party being hosted aboard a yacht. All guests, aside from a few out on the open deck, were inside the main ballroom. It was a bit crowded as the floor had been filled a bit past its maximum occupancy. Over her punch glass, her eyes slowly swayed back and forth taking in everything within her sight. Every guest, both male and female, were luxuriously dressed, accented by the diamond encrusted jewelry they wore. Their fraudulent laughs and smiles drowned out the light Christmas tunes coming from the speakers in the ceiling. Something about it all made Kim cringe.

Everything was red and green, every corner of the floor from top to bottom. Decorations hanging from the walls, tables dressed in bouquets of flowers, candles, ribbons, light fixtures, and of course, the wardrobes of guests, all in the same two colors. She found it all assaulting to the eye, but she herself was wearing an uncomfortably tight red dress for the sake of blending in.

The occupants, the theme, the setting, and overall mood were more than enough to give Kim a reason to pass on the party had she been invited to it. However, she hadn't been invited and she wasn't there for the party.

Kim held in front of her a small photo of a blond man who looked to be about in his thirties. She continued scanning the floor as she gnawed on the inside of her jaw in frustration.

"Where are you?" she whispered behind her punch glass.

"Up towards the front, you see him?" Pedro asked back in a whisper.

"Not yet, might be upstairs," she looked over to the large staircase leading up beyond the floor they were on, "they're guarded though."

At the base of the stairs stood two heavy set men in dark suits and shades.

"I don't think they're gonna just let you walk up there," Pedro said.

"Then we gotta grab everyone's attention somehow."

"Move towards the front, we'll figure something out."

"On my way."

She placed the glass she had been drinking from on the table behind her and took a step forward. She stopped as she felt a hand grip around her wrist. She swiveled her head around and rolled her eyes at the sight of Helena smiling back at her.

She was wearing an extremely short red Santa themed skirt with a hat and matching thigh high boots.

Kim removed her earpiece and closed it in her hand to prevent it from picking up her voice.

"You look ridiculous," Kim said, looking her up and down.

"Well, you look pretty hot." Helena shrugged, looking her over, "See Kim, that's called a compliment, it's when you say *nice* things to people."

"Do you want something or are you just here to get on my nerves like usual?"

"Geez, someone's playing Grinch this Christmas," she smiled, pouring herself a glass of punch.

"Do you have something to say or not, you're giving me a headache."

"Figured you'd have gotten pretty use to those by now." she smiled, "Hey, is it me or is it a little odd that someone would dock a million-dollar yacht anywhere near Joy City? I mean that's just asking for trouble if you ask me."

She took a sip of the punch and flashed a disgusted face. She poured the rest out on the floor and placed the glass down on the table.

"Really?" Kim asked, sucking her teeth at her.

"Needs more sugar," Helena said, wiping her mouth in disgust.

Kim shook her head at her. After nearly eight months of Helena's presence she still found herself in awe of how much personality she had for someone who didn't truly exist.

"Anyway, the guy you're lookin for is over there at the bar," she said pointing, "and you better hurry up cause it looks like he's on the move."

Kim whipped her head around to the bar and saw the man in the photo dressed in a white suit trimmed in black. She quickly put her earpiece back in and rushed in the direction of him.

"He's by the bar, moving towards the stairs, make sure he doesn't get up them," she whispered, pushing past guests in her path.

Pedro didn't answer.

"Hey, you hear me?"

She again got no response.

"Ugh.... Pedro?" she gritted through her teeth.

She was losing her line of sight to the man attempting to weave in and out of the crowd of guests.

"Pedro, where are..." she stopped as a body jumped in front of her.

"Hors d'oeuvres ma'am?" another tuxedoed man asked holding a tray out to her.

"Move!" she huffed at the man, pushing him aside.

She had lost the man's bright head of hair amongst the crowd. She looked over to the staircase leading to the upper deck of the yacht and saw him making his way up. She looked around for Pedro until she finally spotted him in his black pinstriped suit. He was flirting with a female guest on the other side of the floor.

"You've gotta be kidding me," she whispered through clenched teeth.

"He's real focused huh?" Helena said standing next to Kim.

"Unbelievable," Kim growled.

"Here," Helena grabbed an empty glass from a nearby table, "let's get his attention."

She cocked back and hurled the glass through the air with incredible accuracy. It hit the wall just inches from Pedro's head, smashing into pieces.

Pedro, the woman he was talking to, and several other guests stopped what they were doing and all looked at Kim horrified.

"Whoops, guess I was.... or you were a little off target there. Welp, good luck," Helena smiled tip toeing away.

Kim froze and held her hands slightly in the air. Her face turned a bit red and she smiled at everyone trying to break the awkward tension.

"I'm.... I'm sorry, it slipped?" she mouthed to the staring crowd.

She eyed Pedro the longest, discreetly nodding in the direction of the stairs. He nodded back and dismissed himself from the conversation with the woman to join Kim.

"What are you doing?!" she grumbled at him.

"What are *you* doing throwing glass at my head?!" he fired back.

"It wasn't me!" she exclaimed.

"W-what?! I saw you throw it! Everyone saw you throw it!"

"Whatever," Kim rolled her eyes, "listen, he went upstairs. How are we gettin up there? We don't know how much time we actually have."

They both looked over and saw the two men guarding the staircase. Pedro scanned the area urgently and made eye contact with a waiter carrying a tray of glasses filled with champagne at his hip. Pedro took a glass off the tray and motioned for Kim to follow him. He headed straight for one of the men guarding the staircase and purposely tripped himself spilling the drink all over the man's suit.

A collective gasp from all around followed.

"Awww…. sorry man, I..."

Before he could finish apologizing, the man, who was nearly twice his size, grabbed him by his shoulders, lifting him off the ground. A furious look came upon his face as he removed his shades and glared at Pedro.

"Really punk?!" he growled at him.

The other guard took a step over attempting to calm the other down. Pedro then kicked the man holding him up between his legs. He dropped Pedro and fell to his knees. Pedro then attempted to give the other a shove but was barely able to move him. The man grabbed Pedro by his arm and jerked him closer.

He managed to cause a bit of a scene, drawing a crowd who all watched as he attempted to break free from the man's grasp.

"Alright, you're outta here," the man said walking Pedro towards the floor's exit.

The man Pedro had kicked trailed behind them with a slight limp in his step. As the other dragged Pedro through the crowd, they passed Kim. Pedro made eye contact with her and nodded fiercely in the direction of the now unguarded staircase.

"Go," he mouthed to her as he was escorted out.

The commotion had caused such a stir all eyes on the floor had turned in the direction opposite of the stairs. This left Kim an easy opportunity to sneak up without being noticed.

As she quickly sidestepped towards the stairs, she could hear Pedro struggling with the men through her earpiece before she eventually took it out. She tucked her chain into the neck of her dress as she climbed the short flight of royal blue stairs. As she came to the top, the floor split into two narrow hallways that seemed to follow a circular path.

She chose to go left. Cautiously, she walked down the corridor peeking through the window of each door she passed, but all were pitch black inside.

"Hey! What are you doin up here?!" a deep voice came from behind her.

Kim jumped and turned around to see a large man dressed in a suit similar to the men's who had been guarding the stairs. He began walking her down.

"All guests are supposed to be on the outside deck or the main ballroom…"

"Someone needs help in this room!" Kim exclaimed, cutting him off.

"What?" he asked.

"In here, she needs help!" she cried, pointing to the window.

The man walked up, removed his shades, and pushed Kim aside. He looked into the window and shrugged.

"You can't even see in…"

Kim grabbed the back of the man's head and slammed it into the door knocking him out. He collapsed to the floor. She looked up and down the corridor but saw no cameras anywhere. She backed away continuing in the direction she was initially going.

She crept along until coming to a pair of double doors placed in the middle of where the two hallways met completing the rounded corridor. She noticed the door on the left side slightly cracked open. Approaching it slowly, she peeked through the glass and saw their target sitting with his head down at a huge desk placed in the middle of what looked to be an office. He looked to be asleep.

She pressed herself against the wall so she couldn't be seen by the man and knocked lightly at the door. There was no answer. She slowly peeked around the corner looking through the glass again and noticed he hadn't moved from his position. She knocked a bit harder and waited a few seconds but there was still no reaction from him. She knocked again with enough force to be sure she would be heard. She waited, but still nothing. She peeked in and saw him still with his face buried in his arms.

She looked around ensuring she was alone and wouldn't be seen before slowly nudging the cracked door open with her foot. She then poked her head inside and spoke out to the man.

"Excuse me.... sir?" she called.

His head remained down. Kim eyed around admiring the space. Photographs of the man placed all about the room told the office was his. She observed the several plaques, trophies, and awards on display. He appeared to be a very decorated and accomplished man, and wanted everyone who stepped inside the office to know it. She eventually caught sight of an open window to the back left. There were several windows around the office but only the single one in the back left was open. She also noticed just next to the open window a shelf that seemed to be hanging a bit crooked.

Kim turned her attention back to the man at the desk who still hadn't moved an inch.

"Sir, are you OK?"

He remained motionless and mute. Above the doorframe she had poked her head through, she could tell a security camera had been ripped from the wall.

Severed cords hung from a small hole in what would've been a prime place to keep such a camera. Kim reached at her leg under her dress and pulled out her hair pick, releasing the blade. She gripped it in her hands holding it behind her arm and out of sight. She looked around once more before stepping all the way into the office.

"Sir?" she asked again as she slowly began to approach him.

She inched closer and closer towards the man careful not to move too quickly. She rounded to the side in between him and the open window and immediately froze. There was a knife stuck deep into his back. His white suit was stained with blood where the knife had been left.

"What? Seriously?" she mumbled under her breath.

She placed her pick back under her dress and moved behind him. She noticed an open safe tucked under his desk. She knelt down and saw it was completely empty. Swearing to herself, she came back up to her feet and stepped towards the open window to look outside. She looked all around but it was too dark to see anything.

She was completely thrown. She stepped away from the window, placed her earpiece back in her ear, and backed out of the office, making sure to leave the door cracked exactly how she had found it. She quickly began making her way back the way she had come.

"Pedro?" she whispered.

"Yo, what's up?"

"I'm on my way back down," she said.

"You get him?"

"Not exactly, I'll meet you at the car."

Chapter 2

A Gift

"Yep, right in his back, doubt he ever saw it coming," Kim said.

Terrance swore under his breath hearing what she had found on the yacht the night before.

"We took too long, we been so backed up lately. That contract had been sitting there for over a week," Terrance said palming his face.

"We're still not caught up?" Pedro asked.

"Not even close." Terrance confessed, "Did either of you see anyone on the ship who looked like they might've wanted to take him out? Anyone who was eyeing him a little too hard, watching him real close?"

"Yeah, us." Pedro laughed, "I didn't pay anyone else any mind. I don't remember seeing anyone but him head up those stairs either."

Pedro looked to Kim to confirm. She shook her head in agreement.

"Whoever it was had to come in from the window, they definitely weren't on the party deck.

And the kill was way too clean to be done by an amateur. They didn't cover their escape well but looking at it there's no way this was someone who hadn't had at least some training."

"So, he wasn't so much murdered as he was assassinated?" Terrance asked.

"Had to be. Personal gain or contracted, it happened fast and the killer made sure they weren't seen, emptied out a safe behind his desk too."

Terrance and Pedro's eyes grew wide in unison.

Terrance mouthed, "The safe?" to Pedro.

He responded with a slight shrug. They both then turned back to Kim almost as if the exchange hadn't happened.

"Whoa whoa whoa, what was that?" she asked.

Neither of them spoke. She went back and forth staring them down waiting for an answer.

"What was in the safe?" she asked, glaring at Terrance.

He rested back into his chair clearing his throat. Kim turned to Pedro.

"What was in the safe?" she asked again.

Pedro looked at Terrance who gave him a look of defeat and shrugged.

"He was supposedly carrying some bags on the boat. Like three to four-hundred bands worth.... so, we were gonna..."

"You can't be serious." Kim breathed cutting him off, "We were there so y'all could steal the guy's money? Was there even a real hit on him?"

"Yes, that's who told me about the money." Terrance said, "Apparently whatever dirt he had his hands in paid him well enough to rub someone the wrong way. The contract was real but they also mentioned the safe he carried around with him and we just..."

"I don't even care. I'm putting my life on the line for this and y'all aren't even telling me everything? What is that? I guess I was just there to confirm the kill and he'd grab the cash?" she pointed to Pedro, "That's a dangerous game y'all are playing."

Kim despised how money drove both of them. She just couldn't understand it, especially on the part of Terrance. Kim had made enough money from The Pool in her six years to never have to work another day in her life. Terrance had been in The Pool for nearly twice the amount of years she had, and so she couldn't understand him wanting to take any extra risks just for a little extra money.

"OK OK, you're right, that's on us. We shouldn't have did it, we saw what looked like an easy opportunity and jumped at it. It won't happen again, you have my word," Terrance assured her.

Kim looked at Pedro waiting for his apology but he just stood there shamefully staring at the floor.

"Whatever," Kim said, sinking back into her seat.

Kim noticed Terrance had fallen deep into thought. He was staring into space as he groomed his beard with his fingers.

"What's up?" Pedro asked, noticing his focus as well.

"Nothing, it's just, I'm not surprised someone else was after what was in the safe, I *am* surprised that someone actually moved on it though, someone trained too. I'm sure we're the only trained killers in the city, so it must've come from outside JC."

"I mean I could be wrong, maybe it was some gang member off the streets that just halfway knew what they were doing," Kim suggested.

"Maybe, I'mma keep an eye and ear out anyway though. Y'all do the same, I'll let Charlotte and Aaliyah know too. Ain't no other clique of assassins moving in on our city taking our kills, that's all the way out. Last night was their first and last free one."

"Wait, we still get paid for last night though right?" Pedro chimed in.

Kim cut her eyes at him.

"Don't worry, I gotchu both," Terrance assured him.

"Cool, I'mma head out," he said, making for the door.

"Be safe P," Terrance said.

"Always, I'll catch you later Kim," he called over his shoulder.

"Yeah," she called back.

Kim noticed as he abruptly exited, his head remained down, purposely avoiding eye contact with her. He knew she was upset with him; they had been partners for too long for him to be withholding any information from her like he had. She had been too loyal to him and had trained him better than that. She looked back towards Terrance. They made quick eye contact.

"You're not really mad are you?" Terrance asked.

Kim rolled her eyes at his question.

"Never again," she commanded.

"Right, never," he agreed.

Kim slowly rose to exit the room herself.

"Hey, hold up," he said, stopping her.

She turned around and faced him.

"I got somethin for you," he said, reaching in one of the drawers of his desk.

He pulled out a blank manila envelope, dropped it on the desk, and pushed it towards her. Kim stepped forward, hovering over it. It wasn't marked or labeled but she could see from the envelope's thickness that there were a lot of documents inside of it.

"What's this?" she asked.

"I made some calls to some connections I have around the city, had some files pulled, and everything triple checked. I was able to find some information on your folks."

"My *folks?*" she asked, raising an eyebrow.

"Your parents, your *biological* parents. I had someone do a deep scan for everything in the city with your name on it and eventually they came up."

Kim was in shock; she stared at the blank envelope with widened eyes. Terrance waved his hand in front of her face.

"Hey, you good?" he asked

"Yeah.... yeah.... ummm.... thank you, thank you so much," she said, "I really appreciate it, but.... why? After all the trouble looking for them caused a few months ago?"

"Well you asked and I had already started a little digging before all that happened. These past two months you've been on your best behavior so I figured I'd finish up and see what I could find. Consider it an early Christmas gift."

Kim picked up the envelope and marveled at how heavy it was. She was shocked he was able to find anything but was even more surprised that he was able to find a full envelope worth of information. Her mind began sifting through everything she could possibly imagine she might find inside. Names, addresses, pictures; she got goosebumps just thinking about it.

She looked up at him with watery eyes and began to smile. He saw the look she was giving him and knew tears were coming.

"Oh you better not," he said.

Kim threw her arms out and walked around the desk towards him.

"Thank you," she mustered behind a trembling voice.

"Nah nah, don't love me now," he said, blocking her hug, "a minute ago you were ready to bite my head off for lying to you."

"Stop, come here," she cried, forcing a hug on him.

Terrance sat in his chair slightly pulling away from Kim as she embraced him tightly.

"Hug me back!" she moaned through forming tears.

He rolled his eyes but submitted raising his arms around her.

When they finally released each other, Kim wiped her eyes and began staring at the envelope again. Wondering what was inside, what she would find.

"Thank you. Seriously, this means a lot."

"I won't spoil anything for you but there's some answers to a few of your questions in there and a few surprises too, so make sure you're sitting down when you crack it open."

She nodded.

"Be safe Kim," he said, dropping his head down to some paperwork on the desk.

"Always," she said exiting the room.

~

As she drove home Kim found herself distracted. Several things were tugging at her brain all demanding her attention. The city itself was something she always found interesting around Christmastime. How noticeably different it became around the time is what intrigued her most. While nothing disappeared, the crime, hatred, and overall bad aura that normally filled the city seemed to at least drop off a bit.

Glancing out her window she saw couples and small groups of three or four huddled up talking amongst the sidewalks. A normally rare feat. As she passed by the old basketball courts she saw several more kids scattered about the courts than there were usually. A large sign had been posted on the front window of one of the city's most popular grocery stores advertising free hot chocolate.

It happened the same every year, for as long as she could remember, come the first of December the city changed. While it only ever seemed to last for the month, eventually returning to its normal rotten atmosphere by the top of the new year, the change was one worthy of notice. She wondered if it was truly the Christmas spirit getting into the city or just the cold air outside.

Her mind then switched to the mystery aboard the yacht the previous day. She tried to recall anything or anyone suspicious she might have not paid enough mind to while they were there, but nothing came to her. For the man to be taken out so quickly, so clean, yet for so many mistakes to have been made on the part of the killer; it all brought a small shiver to her spine.

Just as quickly as the thought of the prior day's events came, it passed. Out the corner of her eye she saw the faded yellow envelope Terrance had given her resting in her passenger seat. She honestly didn't even know what to think of it. She wondered would there be horrors or delights to be discovered upon opening it. She wasn't completely sure of every reason why but just thinking about either of the possibilities made her incredibly anxious.

The secrets Terrance promised captivated her the most, but again she was torn between thoughts.

Were they good secrets or bad ones? Was whatever what was inside worth knowing, was she capable of handling it? She could feel herself getting hot.

She turned the cool air up inside the car and took a deep breath as she tried to clear her mind of everything clouding it.

Calm down Kim, don't freak out, don't do anything stupid she said to herself.

She fell into a mellow meditative state, repeating the words over and over again in her head. She eventually closed her eyes completely and began to hear the words flow without her having to speak them aloud.

Suddenly several car horns sounded at once and her eyes immediately opened. Just a few yards away a young boy holding a ball stood in the middle of the road directly in front of her. She gasped, and immediately slammed hard on her breaks stopping just a few feet from the boy. He turned around clueless, hearing the screeching sound her tires had made against the road.

A woman, Kim assumed to be the boy's mother, rushed into the street, picked him up, and shot a horrifying glare at Kim through her windshield.

"Are you blind?! Pay attention to the road!" the woman screamed at her.

She carried her son away and continued along the sidewalk directing a vile sideways stare in Kim's direction. Kim's heart was beating violently inside her chest. She began to blush knowing she was being judged by everyone in sight of her. And just that quickly there went Joy City's new peaceful merry air.

She cursed herself for being so careless as to close her eyes completely in the middle of a busy street. A vital mistake she so often made that she had yet to conquer; thinking with her eye's closed, unable to see the things right in front of her.

~

"Can I read it?" Helena asked.

"No," Kim responded.

"C'mon I'll read it out loud."

"No."

"Well, when are you gonna read it?"

"I don't know."

"Well, you are gonna read it, right?"

"I don't know!"

"What?! Kim?!"

"I don't know, OK?!"

Kim leaned against the kitchen counter over her tea and took a deep breath. During her drive home her initial joy and excitement over what Terrance had given her transformed into doubt and fear. She no longer knew if she was comfortable with opening the envelope. She simply didn't trust herself.

"Kim, two months ago this information was the only thing you cared about. Now you have it right here in front of you and you don't know if you're gonna look at it?"

"Yeah, and two months ago caring about it put my daughter and sister's lives in danger."

23

"OK, but that doesn't have to happen again though."

"But it could."

"Kim it's just an envelope, what do you think's gonna happen, a bunch of ninjas are gonna jump out and try to kill everyone you love?"

She looked down into her glass of tea and stared at her reflection. She took a spoon resting on the counter and began swirling it around inside the glass. She watched as the clear image of herself rippled into an unrecognizable mess. She was torn, she wanted to but just didn't have the faith in herself to take whatever she found inside and act rationally with it. She was also just a bit afraid of what she might find inside. She remembered Terrance's words before she left the pool hall.

...some answers...

...a few surprises too...

She couldn't help but wonder. The unknown had driven her mad for so long. The desire to know rather than be forced to guess and assume had plagued her mind for years, begging to be acknowledged, to be sought after. She thought after the events of two months ago she had kicked the desire and convinced herself that she had everything she needed to be happy. Yet, the envelope resting in the middle of her table forced her to second guess her decision to move on from her past obsessions.

She suddenly caught a yellow object creeping into her peripheral vision.

"C'mon, you know you want to..." Helena sang as she waved the envelope in front of Kim's face.

"Enough," Kim said as she snatched it from her.

She placed the envelope back at the center of the kitchen table and fired an annoyed stare at Helena sitting on the countertop. She smiled back and shrugged pleading her innocence.

The sound of keys jingling just outside the front door grabbed both their attention. The door swung open as Cindy and LuLu walked inside. Kim stepped out of the kitchen to meet them after giving Helena one last side eyed stare.

"Hey sweetheart," she said, kissing Cindy's forehead, "hey Lu, how was the mall?"

Cindy and LuLu had gone out shopping together enjoying their holiday break from school.

"Crowded and a mess," LuLu responded, "last minute Christmas shoppers everywhere, should've known."

"Yeah, same crowd every year Lu," Kim laughed.

"You'd think for once people would just get their Christmas shopping out of the way on time," Cindy said removing her coat.

"Doesn't work that way kiddo, never has. Here, let me see that," she said, reaching for her coat.

Cindy handed it over and Kim stepped toward the coat closet.

"I got some tea in the kitchen if y'all want any," she said.

"No, gross. It was bad enough before, but now you don't even heat it up," LuLu frowned.

Kim scoffed at her comment.

"If you tried it cold you'd probably like it."

"I did, that's exactly why I don't."

Kim rolled her eyes.

"Alright well..."

Kim opened the closet and two duffle bags tumbled out spilling several wads of cash onto the floor. Kim sucked her teeth before looking up to see LuLu eyeing the cash. She looked terrified, like she had seen a ghost.

"Hmph.... someone's been busy," Cindy smirked.

Cindy had a way of making light of Kim's work whenever it was brought up. She would crack jokes or poke fun at the act as though it wasn't as serious as it actually was. LuLu on the other hand was still not as comfortable with her knowledge of the matter.

"Hey!" Kim scolded Cindy under her breath, "Upstairs."

Cindy sucked her teeth and headed up. Kim watched her until she made it all the way and turned the corner. She then turned back to LuLu who was still staring speechless at the money resting at her feet. Kim bent down and began shoveling the money back into the bags. She tossed them and Cindy's coat back in the closet and slammed the door shut.

Kim and LuLu traded gazes of anticipation. Hoping the other would speak first and kill the silence.

"Is.... is all that from..." LuLu began.

"Let's not..." Kim said, shaking her head.

"Right..." LuLu nodded.

For two people who were as close as they were, who had known each other as long as they had, moments of awkward silence had become almost routine when they spoke to each other.

The past two months had been an odd pair for them both. After Kim's confession to LuLu it seemed as though they were in a constant struggle attempting to relearn each other and reevaluate their entire friendship. Their conversations were much drier than usual, things just felt different. LuLu's response to Kim's confession had gone about as well as she could've hoped, a complete disaster, nowhere near as well as confessing to Cindy had gone.

LuLu was very outspoken in her distaste for what Kim was doing and she let her know nearly every time they spoke. Whether flat out condemning her or taking light jabs here and there she wasn't shy about making it known that she didn't approve. She was still fearful for her own life after being kidnapped by the 45s, but being as selfless as she was raised to be, she feared for Kim and Cindy's lives even more.

Every opportunity she had she attempted to talk Kim out of it, telling her it's not what her foster parents would have wanted, and never forgetting to emphasize the legality and danger of it all. Points that had all become trivial to Kim, things she had already long hashed out within herself. Whenever it was somehow brought up she always did her best to deflect LuLu's attention from it and change the subject entirely. She hoped that if she could refrain from ever talking about it with or around her she would eventually just forget it and things could go back to normal again. Wishful thinking on her part.

Since her confession Kim had caught her staring at her in ways she never had before, being a bit quieter when they were together than she normally was, and overall just not being the same person she had grown up with for so many years. It was heartbreaking to her. She hated that things seemed like they would never be the same between them again but she also understood LuLu's position. It was a tough pill to swallow. Above all else she was just grateful that LuLu chose to continue even speaking to her and honored her request to keep quiet about it all.

"Ummm.... thirsty?" Kim asked.

"Sure, anything but that tea," she smiled following Kim into the kitchen.

Kim passed Helena on her way to the fridge and flashed a stressed expression. She giggled in response.

"Your Christmas decorations are usually up by now. Are you not putting them up this year?" LuLu asked, taking a seat.

Kim pulled a pitcher of water from the fridge and began pouring LuLu a glass.

"Nah, honestly it's more of a hassle than anything at this point. We just finished getting this place cleaned up from the break in so I'd rather not go putting up some decorations just to take them back down in a week, that'll just be more cleaning up we'll have to eventually do. I bought all that stuff when I adopted Cindy, but she could care less about it really.

I've only been putting them up in recent years just cause that's what normal people do, I guess."

"Which you're not..." LuLu whispered.

Kim froze and turned around just enough to see her face. LuLu was staring at the wall as if she hadn't just said what she had. Kim decided not to comment on it. They'd had several wars of words over the subject in the past two months. She simply wasn't in the mood for another. She turned back around and continued pouring.

"Yeah.... right, so how's school going?"

"It's school I guess, still struggling in just about all my classes, still up to my neck in debt, and I'm only sinking in deeper. Just had to take out another loan."

Kim had to bite her lip to keep from saying something. She was tired of hearing how she was so in debt, in such need of money when all she had to do was ask and she would pay her way through college without a second thought.

"Well, I know you'll get through it, let me know if there's any way I can help."

A response she had uttered countless times. She placed the glass of water on the table in front of LuLu.

"Thanks."

"Mmhmm."

Kim walked back to the counter and poured two glasses full of tea. She pushed one across the countertop towards Helena who thanked her silently with a smile. Kim then walked over with her own and took a seat at the table across from LuLu.

"So, what's been goin on?" LuLu asked.

Kim took a deep breath as she eyed the envelope lying in between them. She debated whether or not to share the contents with her, but she figured it was a better subject matter than what was currently in the air.

"Ummm.... a friend of mine from the office I use to work at did some research on me and my family. I think they might've found my parents," she said, pointing to the envelope.

LuLu looked at Kim with wide eyes.

"Th-that's great, your real parents right?" she asked.

"Yeah."

"So they found out like where they live, their names and stuff?"

"I'm assuming all that's in there."

"You haven't looked yet?"

Kim shook her head behind her glass.

"Why not?"

Kim closed her eyes and shivered. She placed her glass down and gave LuLu a concerned stare.

"Lu, I can't..." Kim said.

"You can't?"

"Lu, chasing my parents.... you and Cindy..."

LuLu breathed a deep sigh before speaking.

"Kim, c'mon, if anything, that situation proves how bad you need this, how bad you want it."

"I don't think I do though. I don't think I want it, not anymore."

"Yes you do." she reached across the table and placed her hand on Kim's, "Listen, that situation is in

30

the past. Two months ago you were practically dying to know them and now everything you need to know is handed to you in an envelope and you're not even going to open it? Kim that's crazy."

It meant a lot that after everything she had put her through chasing her parents, LuLu still pushed her to open the envelope, making no mind of any consequences. She knew it was what Kim truly wanted and she wanted it for her.

"I just don't wanna put anyone in danger again."

"Who says you will?"

"I tried to tell her Lu, but she's hardheaded, she never listens to me," Helena teased from where she sat.

Kim bowed her head in defeat.

~

A humped grassland that rose high, peaked, and rolled out to a cliff overlooking the city. Lush green grass covered the land along with a single oak tree that stood tall providing shade on the hottest summer days. The Hill, Kim called it; Joy City's highest vantage point that gave a breathtaking view to anyone who stood upon it.

Kim stood just a few feet from the edge looking out. She watched as people so far below her walked up and down the sidewalks, and cars drove up and down Joy City's many streets and avenues.

Climbing The Hill was something she did regularly when she was younger. It was where she found the most peace. So high up she could barely hear the sounds of the busy city below her, just the wind whipping the leaves of the tree canopying over her.

It had been a while since she had made the climb up. When she was younger, it was one of the spots she would come to often when running away from The Home. She loved how secluded it was. She could recall a few nights sleeping under the tree overnight. She knew the last time she had made the climb was surely a time before she had adopted Cindy, making her last visit at least five years ago. Yet, the view hadn't changed aside from looking down on a few freshly painted buildings or newly planted trees.

It was what she needed, something familiar. The cool air brushing past her, gently blowing her hair and the tail of her scarf away from her body. She found a peace so calming she could've nearly fallen asleep where she stood. But as always when she found peace, it was soon to be shattered by a sudden splitting headache.

"Geez! Wanna keep a more horizontal path next time K? That climb is steep!" Helena cried as she gasped for air.

She was slowly crawling up from behind Kim on her hands and knees. Once she was next to Kim, she collapsed near her feet and rolled over onto her back.

"Whew!" she breathed, "That walk down is gonna be brutal, I might just jump."

Kim ignored her, still staring off into the distance.

"Hey, what's up K, you good?" Helena asked.

"What are you doing here?" Kim returned.

Helena propped herself up on her elbows.

"Good question, what *am* I doing here? You must have something on your mind."

Kim took a long blink as she shook her head. Helena looked up at her from the ground, waiting.

"Gotta be somethin, I didn't climb up here for fun."

Kim took a quick glance down at her before quickly looking away again.

"Still tryin to decide whether you're gonna open it or not huh?" Helena asked.

Kim closed her eyes and turned her head further away trying to ignore her.

"C'mon talk to me K, remember I'm up here," she pointed to her head, "I already know what's on your mind but you gotta say it first. Think of it as just having a talk with yourself. That's all I am, just an extension of you, your mind rather."

A fact she often forgot as Helena had begun to feel so real to her over the past eight months. Kim looked down at her and opened her mouth to speak but hushed herself before any words came out. She looked back away from her and sighed deeply.

"Should I?" Kim asked, quickly peeking down at her.

"*Should you?*" Helena smiled.

"Please, I don't have the patience for your vagueness right now. I need a straight answer or you're no help to me."

Helena rolled her eyes and fell back flat on her back. She placed her hands behind her head and kicked her foot up on her knee in a lounging position. She closed her eyes and smiled as she spoke.

"Kim, do what you want. Don't let what happened two months ago handicap every decision you make going forward. Especially not this one. No one got hurt, well.... no one we care about anyway, and everything is back to normal. Forgive yourself for whatever you think you did or didn't do. You're smarter now, you don't have to make the same mistakes twice and you won't. You might've been able to convince LuLu that you don't need it, that you don't want to know, but I'm inside that head of yours in ways no one else is and I know better."

"But what if what's inside that envelope is something I'm not ready for?"

"Ugh…. déjà vu, didn't we have this same talk two months ago? What major change in your life have you ever been ready for? What prepared you for your foster parents' deaths? What prepared you for what Joey told you? What prepared you for having to watch him slit his own throat? It's the unknown, you're not supposed to be ready for what's inside that envelope but be ready to accept whatever is. And whatever is inside just know you can handle it."

"Do you know what's inside it?" Kim asked.

Helena's face twisted a bit at her question.

"I'm not psychic Kim," she laughed, "I only exist in your head. I won't know what's in it until you do."

Kim closed her eyes and again began to imagine what could be inside. Wondering would she be filled with joy or sorrow by the time she thumbed through it all. Would she have a visit to plan somewhere or more fuel to add to the mourning of those she couldn't even remember. She also pondered what the surprises Terrance had warned her about might be.

"I can hear your thoughts Kim," Helena whispered, "you're thinking way too hard about all this. Overthinking actually. Stop psyching yourself out. It's the season of kindness and giving, so be kind to yourself and give yourself something nice, give yourself something you want."

Kim repeated her words in her head.

...give yourself something you want.

She had come so far in her life, gotten so used to what her life was she couldn't help but reject change. Change hadn't been kind to her since she was adopted twenty years ago. She glanced back down at Helena, eyes closed, still kicked back lying in the grass with a huge smile on her face.

...give yourself something you want, she repeated again.

Chapter 3

Spared

"Uhhh…. Morning?"

Kim jumped in her seat at the sound of Cindy's voice. She looked up at her, rubbed her eyes, and groaned.

"Ugh…. morning sweetheart. I didn't hear you coming down."

Cindy frowned and moved closer to Kim and stared into her eyes.

"Are you OK? Did you sleep last night? You got huge bags under your eyes," she said.

"Barely…. I'm fine though," Kim pushed herself up from the table, "you want some breakfast?"

"Uhhh…. can you cook breakfast?" Cindy asked, "You look like you need some more sleep first."

Kim had spent all of the previous night and most of the morning tossing and turning in her bed until she came downstairs. She eventually fell asleep at the table after hours of thought. She couldn't help but overthink, no matter how hard she tried not to.

"Yeah, I'm fine. Old as you are though, you should be cooking for me by now," Kim said.

"Teach me," Cindy shrugged.

Her answer surprised Kim. She didn't believe she would've cared to learn but the thought of them bonding over the act excited her. She smiled and nodded.

"OK, I will, maybe later this week, not today though. I gotta head somewhere. In fact, I'm already late," she said glancing at the clock.

"Where are you goin?" Cindy asked.

They immediately made eye contact. Kim saw the innocence in her stare. She quickly glanced over at the table where the envelope still rested unopened. Kim hadn't mentioned its contents to her, she wasn't so sure she wanted to. She looked back at her and saw she was still waiting for an answer.

"Uhhh.... I just gotta.... go..." she stuttered.

Cindy gave her a small smirk and chuckled a bit to herself.

"Never mind..." she said, rolling her eyes as she made for the living room.

She knew Kim no longer had a job, she knew she wasn't one for hanging out with others, and she knew she really had no other place to be so early in the morning.

"Wait wait," Kim stopped her.

She placed her hands on her shoulders and looked at her through worried eyes.

"Are you OK? I realize I probably don't ask you that enough and we don't really talk enough about..."

"It's fine, I'm fine, and you ask me if I'm OK more than enough, too much actually. I promise I'm fine," she laughed gently brushing Kim's hands from her shoulders.

She continued into the living room. Kim watched over her shoulder as she sunk down into the couch and turned on the TV. The way she so easily laughed off the subject still struck Kim the wrong way. She felt guilty. As if her doings had inadvertently corrupted her to a point of feeling numb to the act of murder. The thought resonated horribly with her.

After being kidnapped from her own home and held in a strange place overnight she only seemed shaken up for a few days. After which she was back to normal, making jokes and poking fun at the fact that her legal guardian was a killer. Kim didn't know what to do; be happy that she was so OK with it all, or be horrified by it.

~

Kim pushed through the door to the pool hall and waited to be greeted by Terrance's voice from the back room. She could see the door was open and heard hushed voices speaking from inside.

With the envelope in hand, in the same condition it had been given to her the day before, she walked to the door and peeked inside. She gently knocked on the door and pushed it open. Terrance and Aaliyah were sitting around the desk inside the room staring at an open laptop.

"Hey, am I interrupting something?" Kim asked.

"Nah, actually glad you're here, got somethin you should see," Terrance said, nodding at the screen.

Kim made her way around the desk and stood behind them. She looked at the screen and saw what appeared to be black and white footage from a surveillance camera.

"What is this?" Kim asked.

"Dockyard footage of the yacht you and Pedro were on Sunday. We managed to get it before anyone else got to it." Terrance told her, "Run it back Aaliyah, watch right here."

He pointed to the top deck of the yacht. A window opened and a slender figure in dark clothing stepped out carrying a small black bag. The figure was slim and cut.

"That's a woman," Kim noted.

After clearing the window she pressed her back against the side of the yacht and froze. She began frantically looking side to side. She looked unsure of her next move. After scanning from left to right a few times she eventually shoved the bag into a small waist pack she was wearing and dove off the side of the yacht and into the water.

"Well, she's definitely not trained well whoever she is," Aaliyah said, "didn't cover her escape at all. Left the window open, left the weapon..."

"But she's no amateur either. The kill was clean otherwise, no signs of a struggle. I doubt he even knew what hit him," Kim said.

"Look, I don't care who she is or what kind of training she has. She's killing our contracts, and soon, that's gonna hit our pockets. We're not havin that. Keep your eyes open, if you see her creepin around another target, take her out first," Terrance told them.

They both nodded as they watched the tape over again.

"It's crazy, figured we were the only killers in JC that weren't just gangbangers doin it off the streets," Aaliyah said.

"Well, we lagged on it. Whoever put the hit on him probably got tired of waiting on us," Kim said.

"Think she's solo?" Aaliyah asked.

"I doubt she's with anyone. She doesn't look comfortable enough to be out there alone if it could've been avoided," Kim responded.

"I don't care who she's with or where she came from, just get her out my city," Terrance barked.

"We got her boss man, don't trip," Aaliyah assured him.

"Good," he turned his attention to Kim, "what's up?"

She held up the envelope for him to see. His eyes grew a bit.

"Aaliyah, give us a minute," he said to her.

"Yep," she stood and made her way out closing the door behind her.

Kim sat down in the empty chair and took a deep breath. She held the envelope out to Terrance. He returned a confused stare.

"I mean, you can keep it if you want, I don't really..."

"I didn't open it."

"What? Why not?"

"I just, I couldn't do it?"

"Do what?"

"Take that risk again. Things almost got really bad last time because I was so obsessed with finding them. I don't want that to happen again."

Terrance took a deep breath as he carefully searched for his next words. He knew her too well; he could see in her eyes how torn she was.

"I'm sorry," Kim said, "I really appreciate all the work you did and the information and everything, but I just don't know that I wanna risk putting the people I love in danger like that again you know?"

Terrance leaned close to her gently pushing the envelope back to her.

"Kim, I *really* think you ought a take a look. There's some stuff in there I *really* think you'd wanna know."

Kim watched his demeanor as he insisted. She could see it in his eyes, he wanted her to look, he was practically begging her to. Thoughts began running rampant through her mind. She wondered if he was overselling what he knew, or was it possible he was underselling it? Could there be consequences to not taking a look, or inevitabilities that came with looking?

Did she care, she asked herself, *did she need it, would anything inside truly make her happy?* It took a moment for her to decide but ultimately, she believed not.

Kim pushed the envelope back.

"No.... I'd rather not."

"Kim, there's a lot of..."

"Please," she begged, "I just…. take it."

Surprised, he stared at Kim sideways as she appeared to be on the verge of tears.

He pressed the matter because he knew what was in the folder, he knew her and what she wanted, and he knew she was dying to know what was inside. He wouldn't however force her to look, even if he believed she needed to. He wanted to make sure she made the right choice for herself, but even more so he wanted to ensure that whatever choice she made she made by herself, with no outside influence. He took the envelope from her and pushed it aside on his desk.

"It's your call kid."

A brief moment of silence lingered between them giving Kim a moment to collect herself. She was shaking. She wanted to thank him yet her emotional state wouldn't allow her mouth to form words, but she was extremely thankful for him.

When he wasn't shunning her for doing something he deemed reckless she appreciated the father like role he played in her life; something he swore to his best friend he would do just before he watched him be lowered into the ground. Having no kids himself he was forced to quickly learn how to speak to, care for, and partially raise a teenage girl. He didn't always nail it in Kim's eyes but he kept his promise to her father and did his best. She would forever be in debt to him for this.

She had joined The Pool because it was what she believed her parents wanted of her, but suddenly she began to wonder if part of it had also been a subconscious feeling that she owed Terrance her life.

"So, you got plans for Thursday?" Terrance asked.

"Just gonna try to spend it with Cindy, nothing much really."

"C'mon where's your Christmas spirit?" Terrance said with a small grin.

Kim stared at him crooked.

"Me? I don't know that I've ever even heard you say the word Christmas," she laughed.

"Eh, not my thing but my mom's been on my case lately about not spending enough time with the family so I promised her I'd spend this Christmas and New Years with her and my pops. I'm leavin out of here tomorrow afternoon and I won't be back in here until sometime after the first of the year, so if you hit me up I might be a little slow gettin back to you, trying to completely detox myself from all this for at least a good week."

"Good, a little vacation from here will be good for you, can't remember the last time I saw you outside the walls of this place."

"It'll hardly be a vacation, I can already hear my mom's mouth now. Pleasing that woman is ten times harder than runnin all this," he groaned.

"Well good luck." Kim laughed, "It's just gonna be a normal day for us. Luckily Cindy's not much into it either, so I really don't have to do anything, she'll be cool."

"You not even buyin her any presents or anything?" he asked.

"We exchanged gifts the first two years after I adopted her and then that just kinda fell off from there. We realized being together and having each other was really all either of us wanted. Plus, since she found out about The Pool and knows we got plenty of money to spare she's started asking for a lot more and I'm sucker enough to keep spoiling her. She's got everything she needs and wants already."

"And she's fine knowing where the money is coming from?"

"She could care less, which is honestly both a blessing and equally horrifying to me. I don't know, I just feel like a teenager should have a stronger reaction to finding out their mom is an assassin, I know I did. That's a heavy thing to bear."

"Hmph…. speaking of, how sure are you that she's gonna continue to keep quiet? I never liked you coming clean to her about all this, her or the other girl."

"Relax, they're both fine. I talked to them both and they swore the secret was safe with them."

"Kim, If I bet my life on every time someone swore something to me, I'd have died a couple times in this life already."

She hated how dramatic he could be at times.

"I promise, they're fine, don't worry about it," she assured him.

"Alright," he shrugged, "don't make me regret trusting you."

The doubt in her assurance oozed from his response but Kim paid it no mind.

"What about the rest of the day?" he asked.

"Nothing, need somethin though, a distraction or somethin," she said.

"Well, all we got is contracts here, so unless you want one of those, can't help you."

Kim bit her lip and looked to the ceiling thinking for a moment.

"Sure," she shrugged, "whatchu got?"

Terrance froze in place and looked at her in awe.

"*Sure?* You want a contract?" he asked.

"I need a distraction and honestly it's been the most consistent thing in my life for the past six years that I'm actually good at. Sure, I'll take it."

His puzzled face told how surprised he was by her willingness.

"OK..." he said muddled, "Well I got one that's been idle for almost two weeks that needs to happen ASAP. Should be an easy kill, can you be ready by tonight?"

"Of course."

"Alright, swing back by in a couple hours and I'll give you the details."

"Alright," Kim pushed herself up from the chair and made her way around the desk.

She began to slip out the door but stopped as Terrance spoke.

"Hey?" he called.

Kim turned and looked at him.

"You sure?" he asked, sliding the envelope along the desk towards her.

Kim stared at it for a few seconds, thinking. The possibilities that a quick glance inside could bring about delivered a mix of emotions to her. She wanted to, badly, but the possible risks terrified her to no end.

Kim it's just an envelope, what do you think's gonna happen...

Helena's question began rattling around in her head. Her fear of opening the envelope came from the fact that she couldn't answer that question. She truthfully had no idea what was going to happen and so, she decided the best thing was to just leave it be. She slowly brought her gaze back up to him.

"Yeah, I'm sure," she nodded.

Terrance raised his hands slightly in submission. He took the envelope and stuffed it inside a drawer on his desk.

"Be safe out there Kim."

"Always."

~

Kim was lying out on the couch attempting to get a nap in before she had to return to the pool hall for the contract. Cindy was lying on the floor in front of her watching TV. Kim pulled out her phone and checked the time. She released a deep breath of air before propping herself up on her elbows.

"Hey Cin, I gotta leave in about twenty minutes." she yawned, "I'mma leave you some money to order a pizza though, OK?"

"Alright," she said.

Kim collapsed back down, closing her eyes, trying to squeeze out another five minutes before she got up to get ready.

"Where you goin?" Cindy asked.

Kim's eyes immediately opened. She sat back up noticing Cindy had sat up herself and turned around to face her. The blank stare on her face was so condemning, and she could've sworn she saw a slight smile peeking out from behind it.

"Ummm…" Kim stalled.

She had gotten past instinctively lying to Cindy when The Pool came up, but she had not yet conquered the ability to just tell her the full truth of where she was always running off to.

"Work?" Cindy offered.

Kim bit her bottom lip and nodded shamefully. Cindy sighed.

"Do you trust me?" Cindy asked.

"Trust you?" Kim asked back.

"Yeah, do you trust me?"

"Of course I do, why would you…"

"It doesn't seem like it," Cindy said cutting her eyes at her.

It was a conversation that Kim had been dreading. One that she knew one day would rear its ugly head.

"Cin.... listen," she said sitting all the way up, "I trust you. I swear I do. If I didn't I wouldn't have told you anything…"

"Then why do you still have such a hard time talking to me about it? You know I know."

"Because Cin, it's still hard. I feel horribly guilty every single day I look at you cause I know *this* is not what you signed up for when you said yes to me. I hate myself for putting you in this situation…"

"You're being hard on yourself over nothing, I told you I'm fine."

Kim covered her mouth and shook her head.

"I can't believe we're having this conversation," she mumbled behind her hands.

"Better than us not having it," Cindy challenged.

"OK," Kim nodded, "you're right. The truth is, yes, I have *work* tonight. I have to go…. kill a man."

She felt horribly guilty as the words passed over her lips.

"Cin, it's not that I don't trust you, or that I'm trying to keep anything from you, it's just difficult to talk about with anyone, but especially you because of two reasons. Number one being your age. No normal teenager is having discussions like this. How on earth you managed to take what I told you so well, I'll never understand, but I need you to know that the way you took it is not normal and is actually terrifying to me."

"Why?" she asked.

"Because no fifteen year old should have to live knowing what you know, have to have gone through what you went through two months ago. You may feel OK and you may even truly be OK but understand this is not a normal life we're living, neither of us. You know I've lost a lot in my life and all that loss has rendered me a pretty cold person. I don't fear much anymore. I've looked death in the eyes so many times we're practically friends at this point, but one thing that still horrifies me every second of every day is the thought of losing you. And two months ago really showed me that I'm not making it too difficult for that to actually happen, and I hate myself for that, you deserve better."

"So why keep doing it, why stay involved if you're afraid of what it could cause?"

"The same reason you didn't run away when I confessed everything to you, the same reason your Aunt Lu still chooses to be associated with us and hasn't turned me into the police yet, love, gratitude, comfort. The people I do it with, they're my family too Cin. They've looked out for me, raised me, kept me sane at times. It's hard to just walk away from that."

Cindy looked away from her. She was contemplating something hard but Kim couldn't call it.

"Well what's the second reason?" she asked.

"That I love you, and nothing is more important than you being OK and safe. When I told you about everything you made me feel OK enough to keep doing it because you ensured me you were OK with it..."

"And I am..."

"But," Kim hushed her, "I've seen things take turns and go south fast in the six years I've been doing this, and I just don't want you to end up like me."

Cindy took another deep breath and met Kim's eyes with her own.

"But what if I want to?" she asked with a devious smirk.

Kim's heart and jaw dropped in unison. Her entire body went numb. Cindy began giggling at her reaction.

"Calm down," she nudged her knee, "I'm joking."

Kim placed one hand over her heart and the other over her mouth. Cindy looked at her widened eyes and laughed at the horrified look on her face. Kim tried not to but eventually couldn't help but join in laughing at herself.

"That wasn't funny, don't you ever say that again..." she tried to be serious but small chuckles managed to break through in between each word.

"Listen," Cindy began, "like I said, I'm fine. I won't lie and say I feel nothing but I accepted what you were and who you were a long time ago before you even told me yourself. At first, no, it wasn't easy, but what I saw was that aside from everything else you had going on you were still that kind, loving person that came into Little Angels and chose me all those years ago. That's why I'm fine. Not because it's not crazy, or because I'm a psychopath…. I mean, I might be, I don't know…"

Kim laughed at her.

"…. but I'm fine because to me you're not some crazy murderer or whatever, you're my mom, and I love you."

Kim almost began to cry. In some horribly twisted way, her words were comforting and served as the final assurance she needed that Cindy was in fact OK.

"Love you too kid." she smiled, "I can't promise you I'll ever get comfortable speaking it aloud but I promise I'll try to do better."

Cindy nodded.

"But no more jokes OK," Kim added.

Cindy proudly smiled.

"Almost gave me a heart attack," she said playfully kicking her.

~

"Uhhh…. most unique kill?" Helena asked.

"Unique?" Kim asked back.

Kim was in her bathroom in front of the mirror as Helena sat on her bed.

"Yeah, somethin fun, you know, somethin that was like straight out of a movie."

"I don't know," Kim said.

"You gotta have one, c'mon."

"Ummm…. I mean there was this one…"

"Tell me, I need to hear it," Helena smiled.

"Young guy, inherited a fortune and was basically stomping on everyone he believed was beneath him and it rubbed someone the wrong way. It was probably around kill number twenty for me, something like that. He was in Joy City trying to buy up some land or something and stopped at a restaurant to eat with some of his people. I got there, batted my eyes a few times to grab his attention, and he came over and sat with me. I flirted with him a bit and he let it slip he was deathly allergic to strawberries. So, I had a few strawberry margaritas, got him outside, and kissed him. His throat started closing up and he was dead before anyone got to him."

"Mean," Helena smiled, "man, I wish I'd have been there for that one."

"You got issues," Kim shook her head.

"Hey, you did it not me. If I got issues, you do too."

"Whatever, get off the bed so I can make it up," she called over her shoulder.

Helena hopped off the bed and stood behind Kim in the bathroom peeking her head over her shoulder.

"So what's the plan for tonight? You brute forcin it or going tactical?" she asked.

Kim looked over her shoulder staring at Helena, and then back at herself in the mirror. She noticed the absence of Helena's reflection in the mirror. She had noticed it a few times before but never thought to ask.

"Hey, why don't you have a reflection?" Kim asked, pointing to the mirror.

"Not real, remember?" she responded.

"Yeah but..."

"Your eyes and brain can lie to you all day long but a mirror can't, it can only show you what it sees, what's directly in front of it."

"Hmph…. I guess that makes sense."

"That, or I'm a vampire," she smiled.

Kim cut her eyes at her and gently elbowed her away. A slight buzzing sound suddenly grabbed her attention. Kim peeked out the bathroom door and saw her cell phone going off. She walked over and saw it was Blake calling. She picked it up and answered.

"Hey Blake, what's up?"

"Nothing much, just calling and checking on you," he said.

"I'm good, Cindy's good, we're makin it."

"Cool, wanted to also know if we were gonna see you tomorrow night."

"Tomorrow night? What's happening tomorrow night?" Kim asked.

She could hear him breathe a disappointed sigh through the phone.

"The Home's Christmas banquet? You know the one you missed the past three years that you promised you'd make this year?"

Kim could hear the displeasure in his voice. With so much happening she had truly forgotten she had made the promise to him and Ms. C to attend this year.

"Awww.... Blake I'm sorry I.... things have just been so crazy it just slipped my mind."

He exhaled deeply again.

"You said you'd make it, Ms. C's expecting you and Cindy this year."

"I know I just.... the past few months have just been crazy. I lost my job, my house got broken into, and it's just been one thing after another."

"Do you even go back anymore? You know those kids need us. Remember we were in their same position years ago? Remember all the kids who were there before us and how often they use to come back, always making sure we were good, making sure we had everything we needed? And you know Ms. C and the staff need help."

"I know I know, but..." Kim began.

"No buts," Helena interrupted, "they wanna see you, go!"

Kim shushed her out loud.

"What?" Blake asked through the phone.

Kim froze as Helena laughed at her mistake.

"Nothing, ummm.... look, me and Cindy we'll do our best to swing by OK?" Kim offered.

"OK," he said softly.

She could still hear the disappointment in his voice. She could also feel a hint of doubt; he didn't believe her.

"Same place as always right?" she asked.

"Yeah, seven o'clock," he said.

"OK, I'll try. I promise I'll try. I gotta go, I'll talk to you soon though."

"Alright, love you Kim."

"Love you too."

She dropped the phone hard on the dresser and groaned.

"Hey, what's up? Why don't you wanna go, why don't you wanna celebrate with your people?" Helena asked.

"The energy at those banquets, I just.... ugh."

Kim began to sloppily make her bed.

"What's ugh?" she asked.

Kim turned around to face her.

"Am I wrong? It just gives me a really empty feeling seeing all these families blossoming from this place, yet mine's gone. All the merriment and happiness, and I'm just there, and.... I don't know..."

"Wow.... you really are the Grinch," Helena whispered.

Kim shot her a dead stare.

"I swear, if I knew how to kill you..." she said straightening her sheets.

"Hey hey, c'mon now, none of that. I'm just messin with you." she smiled, "Look, I get it, I do, but at the same time you shouldn't look at it as having to watch other families blossom, look at it as your own family blossoming. K you grew up there, that place is your home, the people in that place are your family. You should be happy they love and want you there so much, some people aren't as lucky. Look at Cindy, her people gave her up because they just didn't want her. Without Little Angel's, without you, she might not have anybody."

Kim stopped, pressed her hands down flat on the bed and gnawed on her bottom lip.

"I know you hate when I'm right, but you know I am." Helena cheesed, "And it may be a bit too soon to bring up right now, but as far as your family being gone, you did choose to pass on your one opportunity to find that out earlier today, so..."

Kim cringed, she would've loved to challenge her but she couldn't. She pushed off the bed and walked over to her closet. She pulled a backpack out, packed a few things inside of it, and walked out the room without another word.

"Cin, I'll be back, I'm going to.... work," she stuttered, passing by her room.

Even after the talk they'd had just twenty minutes prior, work was still the most comfortable term Kim could find to use.

"Well that almost sounded convincing," Helena said, mocking her stammer.

Kim ignored her as she marched down the stairs and up to the front door. She opened it and took a single step outside.

"Kim, wait!" Helena shouted from the top of the stairs.

"What?!" Kim hissed back turning around.

"Can you make me some tea before you go?" she shrugged.

She rolled her eyes and slammed the door shut behind her.

~

Kim was sitting on a bench outside a bar. Night had fallen and the air had gotten painfully cold.

She was dressed in all black, layered as best as she could with a scarf around her neck and her hood pulled tightly over her head, sitting in silence. She was listening for her cue. Amongst the sound of passing cars, pedestrians, and the wind picking up every so often, she remained completely still, waiting.

She then heard the bell hanging just above the door to the bar behind her sound. She quickly eyed a few feet to her right and saw her target walking out. She tucked her chain as she examined the man.

Kim immediately noticed how tall he was, he seemed to be standing about six feet plus a few inches. The black hair on the top of his head fading to grey on the sides gave away his older age.

As he stepped out the door, he waved back inside and started down the sidewalk towards Kim. She dropped her head and waited for him to pass. Once he did and was a few feet down she pulled her scarf up past her nose, stood and began trailing the man. From her side, she pulled a small vial filled with poison, and pulled her hair pick from the other. She released the pick's blade, popped the top of the vial, and dipped the blade into it.

She picked up her pace a bit catching up to the man as he walked. She only needed to break the skin for the poison to take effect. She just needed to be close enough to touch it bare. Her plan was to ask him to speak for a moment and find a way to stick him without him noticing.

She was moving closer, her pick clenched in her fist. She raised her hand ready to place it on his shoulder but suddenly the sound of the bell above the bar's door rang in her ears again.

"Hey, Leonard!" a voice shouted from behind her.

The man turned around and looked. Kim quickly dropped her hand down and stepped to the side to avoid running into him.

"Oh, I'm sorry," she whispered, walking past him.

She looked over her shoulder and saw someone hanging out of the entrance to the bar waving the man down. He stepped out from the bar and began lightly jogging to catch up to the man. Kim rolled her eyes and sucked her teeth, dipping into a small alleyway to her left.

She pressed herself up against the alley's brick wall and began to listen. The two men began walking together in her direction. As they came closer she was able to make out what they were saying.

"I'll have to catch y'all next time. Tomorrow me and my wife are gonna be at a Christmas dinner for the little girl we're adopting," the man she had been trailing said.

"You're adopting?" the other asked.

"Yeah, from this foster home called Little Angel's, been in the city for decades. We walked in there a few months ago and fell in love with this little girl there. We've been visiting her every weekend and we're getting ready to start the adoption process. They're having a little Christmas get together tomorrow, so..."

Kim's jaw dropped and her entire body went limp.

"Ah OK, well next time, you know where we'll be at," the other man said.

"Oh yeah, I'll let you guys know."

The two shook hands and the other man turned back towards the bar. Kim leaned back bracing herself against a dumpster and the wall she was leaning on as the man passed by the alley. Once he passed, she peeked out and watched as he made his way down the sidewalk.

She felt helpless. She looked at the man and thought about her own foster father. She thought about the Christmas dinner he and her foster mother attended just months before adopting her. She imagined how she would have felt that night had they not showed up after they promised her they would. After all the weekends they visited her, she imagined them suddenly disappearing, and her never seeing or hearing from them again.

She then thought about when she did lose them, how empty and hopeless she felt. Being separated from those who she came from, yet managing to find someone who was willing to treat and care for her as their own, only to lose them as well. It was a feeling she wouldn't wish upon anyone, not even her worst enemy, and something her conscience would not allow her to put a child in need through.

She wiped the blade clean of its poison on her jacket sleeve and tucked the pick back at her side. She peaked around the corner to see the man still walking down the sidewalk. She turned and began walking in the opposite direction. She began to wonder how she was going to explain her failure to Terrance. As she looked over her shoulder one last time, her focus was drawn to the top of a building across the street. She saw a figure dressed in black watching the man in a crouched position.

She squinted, focusing hard on the figure and noticed the body was clearly that of a woman. She was eyeing the man like a hawk as he moved down the sidewalk. She took notice to a small waist pack on the woman's side and immediately gasped thinking it to be the same woman from the video she had watched at the pool hall earlier, the same woman who had killed the man on the yacht. She looked back and forth between the man walking and the woman watching him from above. The woman seemed hesitant to act, remaining still, stalking him.

He eventually came to an intersection and turned left out of Kim's sight. Immediately the woman dropped down onto the building's fire escape and eventually to the ground. Without looking in either direction she sprinted into the street crossing in front of several moving vehicles. Three cars slammed on their breaks to keep from running her over. Drivers laid on their horns, cursing her as she made her way across the street and leaped onto the fire escape of another building. She began scaling it, drawing the attention of nearly everyone in the area.

Her actions were abrupt and reckless. She paid no mind to the eyes she drew. This led Kim to believe it had to be the same woman. She began following her. She stayed on the ground, speed walking the same route the man had. She came to the intersection and looked left to see him still walking casually, oblivious to either of his tailers. Kim looked up and saw the woman perched just above him, ready to strike. With a small blade in hand she began leaning forward. Kim quickly removed a small throwing blade from her side and flung it at the woman. It raced through the air but stopped just inches from the woman's face as she caught it bare handed. She slowly turned her head towards Kim. She wore a hood and mask that covered most of her face. Like Kim, only her eyes were exposed and with them she shot a menacing glare down at her.

Kim was surprised she was skilled enough to catch the blade the way she had. The two's eyes remained locked for a brief moment. Kim shook her head no to the woman, warning her to cease her pursuit. The woman stabbed the blade into the edge of the building. She then stood from her perched position and fell back out of Kim's sight. Kim quickly ran to the nearest alley and started up the fire escape after her.

Once she made it up, she saw the woman slowly skipping across the rooftops. Kim immediately began a mad sprint in her direction. Jumping and skipping over small gaps and rises in the buildings, she quickly closed in on the woman. Eventually hearing the sound of her footsteps behind her, the woman turned around and her eyes lit up as she saw Kim charging at her. Before she could react,

Kim tackled her, sending them both over the edge of the roof.

The woman tried to save herself by grabbing onto the edge of the roof but Kim pulled her down with her. They both went crashing onto the railing of the building's fire escape. The woman tried again to save herself, grabbing onto the railing but the weight of Kim hanging onto her was too much, causing her to lose her grip. They both fell crashing onto the cold hard alleyway pavement.

Groaning in pain, swearing under their breaths, they both began trying to pick themselves up from the ground. Kim had landed dazed, just at the woman's feet. Once she realized how close they were she looked up, making full eye contact with her. She was still glaring angrily at her. Kim tried to pounce on her but she reacted quicker sticking her foot out. She caught Kim in her still tender ribs and she collapsed back onto the ground, holding her side. The woman got to her feet and ran, quickly disappearing from the alley.

Kim rolled over on her back writhing in pain. Though they had mostly healed her ribs were still sensitive from the several kicks she had taken to them two months prior. She closed her eyes as she began taking deep breaths, each one causing a sharp pain in her side. She got chills as she laid there. The cold, the pain, the disappointment in herself were all working against her, keeping her from getting up and continuing her chase. She laid flat on her back and cursed herself multiple times.

"You know..."

Spooked, Kim opened her eyes immediately hearing a voice. Helena stood over her looking down with her hands on her hips.

".... for her to be the poorly trained one, you sure seem to be the one on the ground right now," she smiled.

Kim felt a migraine coming over her. She released a breath of exhaustion as she let her eyes fall back shut.

Chapter 4

Two of a Kind

Kim burst through the door of the pool hall and looked around. She saw a bit of light peeking out from the door of the pool hall's back room. She marched over and yanked the door open to find Terrance, Pedro, Aaliyah, and Charlotte inside. They all looked at her through curious stares, noticing her urgency as she entered the room.

"Ran into our favorite assassin tonight," Kim said.

"Who? The woman that was on the boat? Where?" Terrance asked, leaning forward.

"At the bar. She was after the same guy."

"Wait wait, the same chick from the surveillance video?" Charlotte asked.

"Yep," Kim nodded.

"Nah, I don't like it, somethings up, no way she was after the same target as us again," she said.

"Maybe there's more than one ticket on his head, maybe the guy has a lot of enemies," Pedro suggested.

"I could see it happening once maybe but twice in a row in less than a week? No way," Charlotte claimed.

"Yo, what if it's the same person contracting her and us?" Aaliyah suggested.

All five in the room grew quiet as they considered the possibility.

"But why would someone put two contracts on the same person's head though? That doesn't make any sense," Pedro said.

"Unless the first contract was never accepted," Charlotte offered.

"Or accepted too late," Kim added.

Again, they all fell silent.

"We have been backed up lately," Aaliyah said.

"Forget all that," Terrance injected, "what happened? Did you confirm the kill?"

Kim's face went white. She was hesitant to speak, unable to find a believable explanation for her failure.

"I guess that's a no?" Terrance murmured.

She suddenly remembered Helena's words from months ago.

Lies mixed with truth are easier to spin...

"Look, she got in the way. I was there, I had him, but she jumped on me and we went at it for a minute."

"Went at it? Did you at least get her then?" he asked.

Kim again paused searching for another escape.

Terrance sucked his teeth at her.

"Really Kim?!" Terrance woofed impatiently, "You let her *and* the target get away?"

"Look! I was tailing her and she kicked me in my ribs and put me down, OK?!"

"Your ribs?! You told me your ribs were fine a month ago!"

"They are, except when a foot smashes into them!"

"Hey hey, basta!" Charlotte interrupted, "Can you two stop for a second?! You can bite each other's heads off later! We gotta figure this out."

She turned to Terrance.

"Do you have anything else on the guy? Any locations we can find him at tomorrow?"

"No, nothin but the bar he was at last night."

She turned to Kim.

"Were you seen?"

"Not by him, no."

"Did he see her?"

"I don't think so."

"Then he wasn't spooked, there's at least a small chance he'll be there again tomorrow. We'll go stakeout the place and see if we can catch him. And if she shows up we'll make sure she knows JC is ours."

Kim kept quiet knowing exactly where the man would actually be tomorrow. She was still against killing him for the sake of the child he was looking to adopt. She also didn't want any bloodshed near The Home's Christmas banquet. She simply shrugged.

"Well I got somewhere to be tomorrow, you'll have to do it without me," Kim said.

"Somewhere to be? Where?" Terrance asked.

"I have to go be a parent if you must know," Kim snapped back.

They cut their eyes at each other exchanging cold stares.

"Ugh…. you two are impossible." Charlotte whispered under her breath, "It's fine, me, Pedro, and Aaliyah got it."

They both nodded in unison.

"Are you good? You didn't break them again did you?" Charlotte asked, gently pressing on Kim's ribs.

"I'm fine," she said, brushing her hand from her side.

She abruptly turned and exited from the room. She was stomping through the pool hall's common area until Pedro placed his hand on her shoulder and spun her around.

"Hey, you OK?" he asked.

"I literally just told y'all I was Pedro..."

"You know what I mean."

Kim sucked her teeth.

"He's always looking for something to be on me about, I don't get it." she exhaled, "Whatever, I don't care."

He didn't believe her. He knew she often felt picked on by him and it annoyed her to no end. He chose not to press her over it though in fear of further irritating her.

"Alright…. well what's up with tomorrow? You really got plans with Cindy or you just fed up right now?"

"Both actually, our old foster home is having this Christmas thing and they asked us to show up, I promised we'd be there."

"Oh OK, cool. Well we'll handle it then. Probably won't see you again before Thursday so.... Merry Christmas, hope you and her have a good one."

She could tell he was simply making conversation; she knew he cared about Christmas no more than she did. While it was sometimes annoying to her, she appreciated his effort to converse normally with her whenever possible. He always did his best to be not just her pool partner, but her friend as well.

"Thanks, same to you," she said, trying to crack half a smile, "be safe tomorrow."

"Always," he said back.

Kim stepped outside and began walking the path leading back towards the streets. She hung her head low as she walked until a familiar pair of red shoes came into her line of vision. Her head immediately began throbbing. She picked her gaze up from the ground viewing an outfit she had grown too accustomed to seeing.

"You already know what I'm gonna ask," Helena smiled with her hands on her hips.

Kim looked at her unamused.

"Not everyone whose name and face is sent to us deserves to die," Kim said softly.

"I'd say a good ninety-nine percent don't K."

Kim eyed her harshly.

"Hey, I'm not saying you were wrong to let him go but you did lie and withhold some useful information in there to protect him. You know good and well that stakeout is gonna be dead…"

Kim stepped forward, got right in her face, and looked dead into her eyes.

"That kid he's about to adopt, I was that kid years ago, living in that foster home feeling unwanted, abandoned, unloved. At that time, the only thing that made me feel like I was worth anything was the day a couple came in, passed by every other kid, and came and sat down next to me, spent hours coloring with me, reading books with me, came back the next weekend to see me, and then eventually decided they wanted me as their daughter. I won't take that away from that child, cause no matter what that man's done to have someone calling for his head, that child is innocent and deserves to feel loved and wanted."

Kim dropped her head back to her feet as she brushed past a silent Helena.

~

Kim sat up in her bed trying to finish a book she had begun reading a few days prior. She had started and finished three over the past two months without a job robbing her of most of the hours of her days. She was a speed reader, always had been. Once she started a good book she couldn't put it down. She always had to know what happened next. She couldn't wait, she couldn't lay down to sleep without knowing. She suffered enough simply not knowing in her own life, she relished in the freedom to decide herself how quickly things played out, how quickly resolutions were made. She often found herself in envy of the characters in the books she read. They were so lucky to have such a dedicated reader as herself turning the pages of their stories. Their suffering and pain never lasted long in her hands, she always turned the next page, she always read the next chapter.

However, her focus was askew. She couldn't concentrate as her own life's story was currently too murky to indulge in that of a fictional being's. She removed her reading glasses, closed the book, and set it aside on her night stand.

She turned off the lamp resting on the night stand and pulled her covers up over her head. As she laid there she couldn't shake the thought that maybe she had made a mistake, or a couple. Maybe she should've opened the envelope, maybe she should've killed the man at the bar when she had the chance.

She felt like a prisoner within her own mind, bound by bars forged of her own inquiring thoughts and wonders. She longed for someone, something, to just turn the page, read the next chapter, and end her suffering.

~

"I'm getting tea, don't worry," Kim said into the phone pressed between her cheek and shoulder, "ask your Aunt Lu if she wants anything."

Kim reached up and pulled down three boxes of tea and placed them on top of her cart full of groceries.

"She said she's good," Cindy said through the phone.

"Alright, I'm almost done here. Let Aunt Lu know I should be home in like thirty minutes. Make sure you're ready cause we won't have a lot of time before we have to leave once I get there."

"Alright."

"See you in a bit."

"Alright bye."

Kim stuffed her phone in her pocket and resumed pushing her cart towards the front of the store.

It was Christmas Eve, the night of The Home's Christmas banquet. She was dreading it but decided to keep her promise and show up. She also couldn't help but wonder if she would see the man she let go the night before. She was curious about him and his endeavors. In her eyes, he obviously had a great heart for what he was about to do, so she couldn't help but wonder what could have made someone despise him enough to want him dead.

She reached the front of the store and groaned seeing the massively long lines of shoppers standing at each register.

"Seriously?" she whispered to herself.

She picked a line and parked her cart at the end of it. She pulled out her phone and began to text LuLu.

"Long lines at the store, make sure y'all are ready when I get home so we don't end up getting there late."

She hit send and slumped down onto her cart. She was already dreading the night. Just the mere thought of how many fake smiles and laughs she was going to be forced to put on made her sick to her stomach. Standing there she began to wonder if her foster parents had enjoyed the many Christmas banquets they attended with her. She ultimately figured they must have on the account that they never missed one after adopting her.

"Kim?" a voice called from behind her.

She turned around and saw William smiling as he walked towards her.

"Hey, how've you been?" he asked.

"Hey," she smiled back, "I'm good, how bout you?"

"Tryin to make it," he laughed.

"Aren't we all." Kim laughed back, "Good to see you again though, it's been a while."

Aside from a few texts here and there, over the two months since Kim had gotten fired from her office job she hadn't spoken to or seen William since.

"Yeah, last time I saw you, you were storming out the office kicking over vases."

Kim blushed a bit recalling the day.

"Uhhh.... yeah, not my proudest moment. How's Max?"

"I don't know, haven't seen him in a while either actually."

"Is he not at the office anymore?"

"He may be, but I'm not."

"What?" Kim asked.

"They laid off a bunch of people not too long after you left."

"Awww…. Will, I'm so sorry," she said, "where are you at now?"

"Still kinda in between jobs. You know they didn't even bother putting in a good word for anyone they let go. They just kinda left us all out to dry."

"Ugh…. I hate that…" Kim moaned.

"Yeah, you were right about that place, it was no good, you were smart to get out when you did," he told her.

"Well, I didn't get out so much as I was kicked out but…"

"Right," he laughed, "so what have you been up to, where are you at now?"

"Ummm…. I have a friend that's helping me out at the moment, until I can…. you know, get back on my feet. It's hard to find a job to support yourself and a teenager in this city."

"You right about that, I don't know what's gonna happen but I may eventually have to move outta here. I hate to leave my parents here though cause they're getting old and will probably need someone close to take care of them. But unless I can find a job soon, I don't know how much longer I can afford to stay here."

Kim genuinely felt awful for him. To not have the ability to live in Joy City was bad, as Joy City was usually where people came when they didn't have the ability to live anywhere else. This was what the city did to those who stayed in it for too long; sucked them dry and spit them back out into the world with only pennies to their name. Hearing such situations reminded her just how truly fortunate she was to never have to worry about money, regardless of where it all came from.

"Will, if there's a way I can help let me know," she said.

He smiled at her offer.

"I appreciate it but we're in the same boat really. Don't worry about me, I'll figure it out eventually."

"Right.... same boat..." Kim murmured, turning away from him slightly.

She felt up to her neck in guilt for what she couldn't tell him.

"Well hey, I gotta grab some stuff for dinner tomorrow and get outta here before it gets too late, but it was great to see you though," he smiled as he began walking away.

"Yeah, you too," she smiled back.

"And hey, Merry Christmas," he added, turning back around.

"Merry Christmas," she echoed.

As he turned his back to her, the smile on her face turned frown. She sighed heavily, feeling for him in his trying times. While she hadn't seen or spoken to him in a while she still considered him a good friend and hated to hear that he was struggling. She especially hated hearing that he may have to leave his parents alone in the city. She recalled him having mentioned to her before how dependent they were on him and the thought of them having to be without him broke her heart. She could only imagine how tough of a spot both he and they could soon be forced to face.

If she thought she could do it without him raising an eyebrow to it she would have run after him and given him whatever he needed to make it for the next six months in cash. But she knew he would have questions that she simply couldn't answer.

She slumped back down over her cart and continued her wait in line.

~

"Ugh…. Lu come put these in for me," Kim cried from in front of her bathroom mirror.

"You really don't get out much do you? It's just an earring Kim, just stick it through the hole," she laughed.

"The hole feels like it's gotten smaller."

LuLu joined her in the bathroom and looked at Kim's ears.

"It probably has," she laughed.

"What? How?" Kim asked leaning closer to the mirror.

"That's what happens when you don't wear them enough."

"Whatever, forget it," she said, tossing the earrings aside, "we're gonna be late. Is Cin ready?"

"I don't know, I've been in here watching you fight with those earrings for the last ten minutes."

"Ugh…. you're no help," Kim moaned speed walking towards her bedroom door.

"What's wrong, you seem stressed," LuLu said.

"I just don't wanna be late. I already know I'm gonna hear it from everyone there for not visiting enough as it is."

"I doubt anyone we know besides Blake is even gonna be there. No one's gonna say anything anyway though, and Ms. C is just gonna be happy to see you there."

"Still, let's try to be on time," she said, walking towards the door.

"Well, when are you gonna get dressed?"

Kim stopped, turned, and frowned at her. She looked down at her black long sleeved pullover and black jeans.

"What's wrong with what I'm wearing?" she asked.

"Nothing…. I mean it's kinda dark but…" she shrugged.

Kim cut her eyes at her.

"I mean it is a Christmas banquet Kim," she shrugged.

Kim sucked her teeth waving her comment off. She crossed the hallway and raised her hand to knock on Cindy's door just as the doorbell rang. Her focus shifted and she turned away to answer it.

"Cin, we're leaving in five minutes! Be ready!" she shouted over her shoulder stepping down the stairs.

Once she got to the bottom of the stairs she walked up to the door and looked through the peephole. She saw Pedro standing with his back turned at the doorstep.

"What?" she whispered to herself jerking the door open.

He turned around to face her and greeted her with a nod.

"What are you doing here?" she asked, hanging halfway out the door.

"Maybe I just stopped by to say hello, spread some holiday joy?" he said with a slight smirk.

"I have somewhere to be Pedro, I don't have time to..."

"OK OK, listen. I know where the target is gonna be tonight. Searched him online, found some of his pages, he's been posting about some Christmas party thing tonight. I'mma let Aaliyah and Charlotte know and..."

"No! No!" she said in a hushed tone.

Kim looked behind her and stepped outside quietly closing the door. She moved close to Pedro and spoke sternly.

"Don't tell them anything. Listen, that Christmas party he's gonna be at is the same one I'm going to tonight with Cindy."

"Perfect, you'll already be there so you can..."

"No, listen! The party is for the foster home we grew up in. There's gonna be kids around, people looking to adopt those kids, I don't want any blood spilling around there, especially not tonight."

"Well what are we gonna do then?" he asked.

"Nothing! They're staking out the bar tonight right? Let them."

"What are you gonna tell Big Dog?"

Kim shot him an incredibly annoyed stare.

"Pedro, *nothing!*" she said now getting animated with each word she spoke.

"But if we lose him..."

"We lost the last one and still got paid for it, don't worry about it. Just don't say anything OK? We don't need a team of assassins running around a bunch of kids in need on Christmas Eve, we'll take care of it, it'll be fine."

"Alright.... I guess," his voice was timid.

"Look I'm sorry but I gotta go. When I get there I'll find the guy and keep an eye on him, see what I can find out and let y'all know. But don't say anything to anyone, OK?"

"Alright..."

Kim could hear the defeat in his voice. She knew her tone had come off unnecessarily rude and a bit hostile. She regretted speaking to him in such a way and knew she owed him an apology but she was already short on time and patience. She figured she would have the opportunity to give him one later.

"Be safe," she said as she quietly stepped back inside.

She gently closed the door behind her, turned around, and released a distressed sigh.

"Hey! You two, we're gonna be late if we don't leave right now!" she yelled upstairs.

"Alright alright," Cindy moaned, appearing from around the corner.

LuLu was right behind her as they both made their way down.

"Who was at the door?" she asked.

"Carolers," Kim shrugged.

~

"Hmmm…. a lot of people here this year," LuLu said, taking view of all the cars in the parking lot.

"Was it not this packed last year?" Kim asked.

"Not really, the parking lot wasn't this full."

"Great," Kim groaned under her breath.

They had arrived just ten minutes after seven. LuLu parked her car and turned towards Kim noticing she was staring at her.

"How long do these usually last?" Kim asked.

"Varies," she shrugged, "just kinda depends on when everyone decides to get up and walk out."

"Well, I might have about two hours in me," she said, opening the car door.

As they walked up to the banquet hall vivid flashbacks began rushing through her mind. All the years she came with her foster parents, and the two she came with Cindy, all of which were relatively happy memories. The smiles and laughs, whether genuine or not, the small buffet of food lining the back wall that was barely enough to feed everyone, and a few Christmas-like decorations here and there, the imagery was all coming back in floods.

As she footed up the pair of stone steps leading to the hall she got chills. It had been so long since she had been there but it hadn't changed a bit from the outside. She could practically see herself and her parents walking up the steps together so many years ago, all dressed in matching colors. A sort of blissful high came over her stepping on such familiar ground for the first time in years. She then walked inside and her jaw dropped.

The hall had completely transformed from what she had remembered. A stage had been built on the back wall with stairs leading up both sides, the small buffet of food was now two much larger buffets with a much larger selection of food in each. Snow white decorations lined the hall from corner to corner accented with splashes of Christmas red and green. The place looked to have been completely gutted from the inside and remodeled, it was almost completely unrecognizable to her.

"Whoa..." Cindy said, admiring the hall herself.

"This place looks.... different," Kim said.

"Yeah, things tend to look different when you haven't seen them in three years," LuLu said.

Kim also took notice to how many people were present. The hall looked to be filled with twice as many people as she ever remembered seeing in the past. Whether sitting and chatting, or standing in line filling their plates with food, the hall felt more alive than ever.

"Hey, you made it!"

The three looked to their left and saw Blake approaching them with a huge smile on his face.

"Great seeing y'all," he said, embracing all three of them.

"Yeah, you too. This place has really come a long way since we lived at The Home," Kim said, still in awe.

"Oh yeah, some donations over the years let Ms. C dress it up a lot since we were kids," he said.

"I see, it's changed a lot."

"Hey, you see anyone from our group here?" LuLu asked him.

"Well you two makes five now, Rebecca and her little girl are here, and Carter and his family showed up."

"Rebecca had a little girl?" LuLu asked with a smile.

They continued their conversation, but Kim zoned out further admiring the hall. She knew how hard Ms. C worked keeping The Home together and everything she sacrificed in its name. She was happy to see it all paying off. She smiled a bit as she took it all in, happy to see the growth of a place she considered an extension of The Home.

Out the corner of her eye she caught sight of Ms. C kneeling down, fixing the hair of the shy little brown haired girl she had met at The Home two months ago. Kim smiled and made her way over to them. She placed her hand on Ms. C's shoulder. She looked up and her eyes grew wide as a massive smile came over her face.

"Kim! You made it!" she stood and hugged her, "It's so good to see you! Thank you for coming!"

"Of course, it's no problem, I really should've been here the past few years really.... I just..."

"Hey hey hey, I told you about that, stop beatin yourself up. You got older, you gained responsibilities, I understand."

"Thanks," Kim smiled, "this place looks great."

"Yeah, we got so many blessings from so many families, we decided to try to fix it up a bit, make it a little easier on the eyes."

"Well y'all did a great job. I walked in here and didn't even recognize it. I mean it looks totally different from just the last time me and Cindy were here a few years ago."

"Yeah, speaking of Cindy, where is my little angel?" she asked.

"Angel?" Kim smiled, "Are we talking about the same kid?"

They shared a laugh. Kim turned around to see that she, LuLu, and Blake had all vanished from where they had been standing before.

"Well, she and Lu were right over there. I don't know, I'll make sure you see her before the end of the night."

"Of course."

Kim looked down and saw the little girl had tucked herself behind Ms. C's leg.

"Hey there," Kim said softly.

"Hey bug, remember her? She's got the same name as you, remember?" Ms. C asked her.

The girl smiled just faintly enough to show she did remember her, yet she still refused to speak or budge even an inch.

"Still shy as ever," Ms. C smiled.

"But so precious. Do you accept trades?"

They shared another laugh.

Ms. C then looked past Kim and smiled. She knelt down next to the little girl and pointed discreetly.

"Hey look!" she whispered to her.

The girl's eyes lit up with joy as she slowly inched out from behind Ms. C's leg, and happily trotted right past Kim. Kim turned, following her with her eyes and saw the girl walk up to a man and woman who had just entered the hall. Kim's eyes rose from the shoes of the couple to the faces of those in them, and her heart skipped a beat. She saw the tall man she had tailed from the bar the night before.

"Aside from me and a few members of the staff, those two seem to be the only people she trusts. They've been coming to see her for the past few months. They're gonna tell her they wanna adopt her tonight for Christmas," Ms. C explained.

"Awww…. really?"

"Yeah, great people. Super nice."

Watching the man pick the little girl up and trade smiles with her she again couldn't help but wonder what skeletons rested in his closet. He seemed so nice, so genuine, so loving. So much so that he had even convinced Ms. C of this, but she then remembered the unfortunate reality of Ms. C's character. It wasn't hard for anyone to fool her as she attempted to see the good in everyone she met, which often led to her overlooking whatever bad was plainly visible. She saw it in Kim's foster parents who turned out to be assassins, and even still saw it in Kim as she herself was now one.

Regardless of the reason, she was now sure she had done the right thing sparing the man. Seeing the smile he and his wife put on the little girl's face warmed her heart. She refused to be the one who robbed her or the couple of that happiness.

A young blonde woman came and whispered something into Ms. C's ear to which she nodded.

"Hey," she turned to Kim," I gotta run and greet some folks but have fun, get some food, and mingle a little. Becca and Carter are here too so definitely make sure you see them, and let Cindy and Lu know to come find me before the end of the night."

"I will," Kim smiled.

"Good to see you kid," she cheesed, patting her back.

"You too," Kim cheesed back.

She turned and looked back at the little girl and couple. She was happy for them. Seeing them smile and laugh together brought back some of her earliest memories with her foster parents. She specifically recalled the first day they walked into The Home.

She was sitting at a table by herself coloring. Then a soft voice came from behind, greeting her. She turned around and saw her soon to be foster mother bent over smiling from ear to ear. Her foster father standing behind her with the same expression on his face. The memory was so vivid. She could remember the worn out bright pink turtle neck sweater her mother was wearing and the dingy wrinkled white dress shirt her father had on under his thin jacket. Wardrobes she assumed had been strategically picked out to ensure no one passing by would think to give either of them a second look.

Why are you sitting all by yourself sweetheart?
She was so shy she didn't dare speak back.
Don't you wanna play with the others?
She just continued staring at them confused. No visiting couple had ever come up and spoken to her before. She recalled being truly terrified in the moment with two smiling strangers towering over her.

You're shy huh?
She remained mute. Eventually Ms. C walked over and confirmed to them that she was. She then introduced Kim to them better than she could've done herself. It would take two more visits before she would begin to speak to them on her own and five more months before they would ask her if she would like to be adopted by them.

She believed the little girl and her to be much alike, sharing more than just their names. As she watched her smile and laugh with her soon to be family, she could see herself, so many years ago, sharing those same smiles and laughs with her own. It was like looking into a mirror of the past.

She smiled, hoping that she would be as happy with them as she had been with her own foster parents, hoping that that happiness with them would last an eternity longer than her own did.

She looked around until she spotted LuLu and Cindy speaking with other guests and made her way over to join them.

~

The night was winding down, a few guests had already left, and several others looked to be readying themselves to soon leave as well. Ms. C was on the stage at the podium making a speech thanking everyone in attendance. Kim, Cindy, and LuLu had eaten and had a chance to catch up with a few of the guests they knew. While Kim and LuLu only knew a handful of people present Cindy saw several kids she had met while living in The Home and spent most of the night conversing with them. Kim loved seeing that after so many years The Home was still bringing kids together and serving as the birthplace for lifelong bonds to be formed between them.

Kim bit down on a yawn that told her it was time to go. She pulled her phone from her pocket and glanced at the time.

"8:48" it read.

She leaned over and nudged LuLu showing her the phone.

"My two hours are about up," she whispered.

LuLu twisted her lips at her remark.

"Lighten up, the hall will probably close pretty soon anyway. It's not like you have anything else to do tonight."

She quickly glanced at Kim with wide eyes. She raised her eyebrows at her. Kim could feel the judgement in her stare.

"*Do you?*"

Her tone obviously hinting at something.

"No," Kim breathed, placing the phone back in her pocket.

She leaned back in her chair and looked around at all the people who had showed up. The hall was full of families of all colors, shapes, and sizes. She couldn't get over how different it was, how much the event had grown in her few years away from it. It was a truly heartwarming sight to see.

Ms. C's speech came to an end and was met with roaring applause and a standing ovation from everyone in attendance.

"Twenty more minutes OK? If it doesn't look like people are starting to head out, we'll be the first," LuLu said.

Kim nodded.

As the rest of the remaining guests began returning to their seats, Kim noticed the man from the bar the night before remain standing. He whispered something into his wife's ear and she made a gesture towards the exit. He nodded to her before beginning to make his way in that direction.

Kim had an urge to speak to him. She wanted to know more about him, pick his brain, and just see what she could get out of him. What she really wanted though was a reason as to why someone might want him dead.

"I'll be right back, I'm gonna step out and get some air," she whispered to both Cindy and LuLu.

"You better not leave us," LuLu said.

Kim sucked her teeth at her.

"I'm not, I'll be right back."

Kim followed the man outside and saw him crossing the parking lot. She assumed going towards his car to retrieve something. She stood just outside the door of the hall waiting for him to come back.

She looked up at the sky, and noticed how beautiful the night was. It was one of those nights she wished she had time to just sit back and admire the stars. She began to think how amazing the view from the top of The Hill looked. She remembered the nights she spent sitting under the tree when she was younger. The view of the slumbering city was always so stunning to her. She could recall not even sleeping some nights, staying up just to watch the eventual sunrise.

She too often forgot it wasn't Joy City itself but the people within it that gave it its ugly reputation. There was a time, long before she was even thought of, that the city was known as a pleasant point between places. It was truly a shame what it had fallen to. However, there was still beauty to behold in the city. Come nightfall it still had a skyline that could take one's breath away when viewed from the right vantage point.

The man slammed his car door shut and began heading back towards the hall. He had a coat in his hands Kim assumed was his wife's. She quickly began thinking over a few possible conversation starters she hoped could eventually lead him into answering the questions she had about him.

As she watched him slowly cross the lot a flash of light caught her eye. It had come from just above a building to the left of the parking lot. She squinted, focusing on it and made out a blade that the moonlight had hit just right. She followed it up and saw her; dressed in all black, waist pack on her side, the same woman she had encountered the night before perched on the edge of the building.

Kim cursed under her breath, looking back and forth between the woman and the man still crossing the parking lot. He was again completely unaware of the set of eyes on him. The woman stood from her crouched position on the building's ledge.

Kim tucked her chain and quickly peeked back inside the banquet hall. She grabbed a dark scarf hanging from a rack and fashioned it over her head as a hood and mask. She immediately fell into a mad dash across the lot. The woman crossed her arm over her chest lining up her throw. The man stopped cold staring in confusion as he saw Kim sprinting towards him. In an effortless swing of her arm the woman threw the blade aiming for his head. Kim, a few feet from him, dove out of her sprint extending her right hand to shield him. The blade hit her hand and she landed hard on the asphalt.

"Oh my god, ma'am are you OK?!" he asked, attempting to help her up.

She looked at her hand and saw blood dripping from where the blade had hit her. She winced, biting her lip, flexing her hand from the sting.

"You're bleeding, you need..."

"I'm fine." she said, cutting him off, "You need to go inside."

"But are you..."

"Now!" she commanded him.

The man stood nearly a foot taller than her but cowered in the wake of her aggressive tone. She glared at him with fire in her eyes that told him to heed her demand.

"Go!" she yelled, pushing him towards the hall's entrance.

He looked back only once until safely inside.

Kim looked back to the rooftop and saw she was still standing there. Their gazes were locked, anger growing between them both with every passing second. Kim looked down at her still bleeding hand. She pulled her hair pick from her side and cut part of the scarf's end off. She wrapped it around her hand and tied a tight knot on the back of her hand to keep it in place.

Kim looked back up at her as she began to slowly step backwards. She eventually stopped and dropped down disappearing into an alley.

"Alright K, listen..."

Kim looked to her right and saw Helena sitting on the hood of a nearby car.

".... you lose to her this time and I'm switchin to her side. I can't afford to be associated with all this mediocrity," she said, turning her nose up.

Kim ignored her remark. She looked back towards the hall once more before taking off in the direction of the woman's exit.

She slowed her pace to a crawl as she came to the mouth of the alley. The moonlight offered a small bit of visibility. The alley looked to be leading somewhere. She walked it slowly, creeping along as she cautiously looked in all directions around her.

The end of the alley was an open squared off area. She looked around and saw the backs of buildings rising above her, dumpsters lining the brick walls, and fire escapes leading up to the rooftops. She walked to the middle of the opening and spun slowly in place watching and listening. She could feel someone in her presence, she could sense she was being watched but couldn't make out from where.

Still slowly rotating in place, she heard a rustling sound from behind her. She quickly turned to face it, clinching her pick tighter in her hand only to see a small rat crawl from under a dumpster and scurry off.

She exhaled and relaxed her body standing upright. She tucked her pick back at her side but then heard another sound come from the opposite direction. She turned again, staring at another dumpster but saw nothing move. She shifted her gaze up just a few inches to the fire escape hanging above and managed to make out a large black object resting against the brick wall. She squinted hard, barely able to see it with such limited light. She took a few steps forward but froze as the object appeared to twitch.

"What the..." Kim whispered under her breath.

Two glowing spots appeared on the object; a set of eyes. Suddenly it uncurled into a figure; it was her. She quickly rose from her sitting position and jumped over the fire escape's railing. She threw a blade out but Kim avoided it with a short hop backwards. Kim saw it stick into the asphalt at her feet. She then pulled her focus up to see the woman charging at her.

She ran up to Kim swinging with a left hook, a right, and a final uppercut. Kim easily dodged all three. The woman then went for a roundhouse kick with her right foot which Kim ducked. Upon landing back on the ground, she lifted her opposite foot and attempted to stomp Kim in her crouching position. Kim caught her foot and twisted it, forcing her to kick out. This sent her flying back a few feet.

She landed sloppily on her side. The two traded glares before the woman jumped back to her feet and charged Kim once more.

Surprised by her commitment to her street brawling style Kim was caught off guard and tackled by the woman. She lifted Kim off the ground and pushed her back into the brick wall behind her. Kim tried to press her away but couldn't move her. She had her pinned. She grabbed Kim tightly around her waist and lifted her into the air. Kim started to deliver punches to her back trying to get her to let go. She pounded hard on her back three times before the woman began falling backwards and turned over with Kim wrapped in her arms. They landed hard on the asphalt.

Kim was face up with the woman lying on top of her. Kim quickly threw her to her side and kicked her in her stomach sending her sliding away a short distance. She stopped herself and rose to a knee. She then reached at her side and tossed another blade at Kim which she ducked. The blade stuck into the wall behind her. The woman again charged her, swinging another hook. Kim sidestepped, avoiding the blow, and pulled the blade she had thrown out from the wall and slashed at her. She backstepped evading the slash as Kim was thrown off balance by her whiff and punished with an elbow to the face. She dropped the blade as the woman followed with a right hook and a backhanded fist that struck Kim in the mouth. She stumbled backwards setting some distance between the two of them.

They stared each other down for a moment, hot with adrenaline. Kim pulled down the scarf covering her mouth just enough for her to spit out some blood. She quickly pulled the scarf back up and charged the woman herself. She ran up and attempted to deliver a crushing kick to her knee but she backstepped and countered with a jab. Kim blocked it and immediately went into a stance to block another, holding her forearm in front of her face. Rather than jab again, she hooked Kim's arm with her own and pulled it to the side. With her free hand she grabbed Kim's throat and began to choke her walking her backwards into a dumpster. Kim grabbed her wrist and squeezed it hard until she let go. Immediately she again punched Kim in the face and delivered another elbow to her chest. Kim pulled her arm free and used the other to push off of her, creating a small space between them. The woman attempted to close the space again but Kim, using the dumpster as leverage, lifted herself in the air and kicked her backwards a bit. Kim jumped back putting a few more feet in between them.

They were both gasping for air, staring at each other through hateful eyes. Kim was surprised. Although she fought recklessly and without balance, she was more than an average fighter.

The woman pulled another blade from her side and picked up the other Kim had dropped. She rushed toward her again wielding both in her hands. She swung the blade in her right hand but Kim evaded it leaning backwards. Kim then grabbed her arm and pulled her forward throwing her off balance. She placed her foot behind hers and pushed her backwards sweeping the woman off her feet, slamming her to the ground. She groaned in pain for a second before kicking Kim in her ribs. Kim immediately collapsed to a knee holding her side.

The woman rolled back to her feet and growled as she looked down on Kim. She then dropped both blades and pulled a gun from her side and pointed it directly at her. Kim's eyes grew wide as she stared down the barrel. She instinctively rose and kicked the gun from her hand. In one fluid motion Kim pulled her hair pick from her waist and slashed at her arm. The blade cut through her sleeve leaving a large gash on her arm that began to drip blood. The woman stumbled back staring at her wound in shock. While she was distracted Kim charged her, pressing her shoulder into her chest. She slid backwards a bit before collapsing to a knee.

Kim picked up the gun she had dropped, and walked her down with it extended out in front of her.

"Make a move I don't like," she dared her.

The woman bowed her head in defeat. Kim held the gun directly in front of her head. Finally able to catch her breath her mind began to race. As much training as she had in hand to hand combat, she couldn't remember ever having to use it as much as she had to best her. She began to rethink her previous claim that the woman was poorly trained.

She debated shooting her point blank but couldn't help her curiosity. Killing her right then and there would rob her of the opportunity of getting any answers out of her. She believed even Terrance, as much as he claimed he just wanted her dead, would probably want to know a bit more about her as well. Kim looked her over as she gathered her thoughts on what to ask first when something caught her eye. The woman was wearing a black zip up jacket that had a small logo in the top right corner. She immediately recognized it. It was the Atrium logo, the exact same one from the jacket her father wore in the damaged photo of her and her biological parents.

"Atrium?" she whispered aloud.

Her hesitation gave the woman an opportunity to grab her arm, pull her in, and ram her shoulder into her chest. Kim dropped the gun and flew back onto her hands and knees. She cursed herself silently for dropping her guard.

The woman picked up the gun and began slowly walking towards Kim.

"Now, make one I don't like," she said, mocking her words.

Kim noticed a hint of amusement in her voice. She was relishing in the moment, in the position she had her in. Kim bowed her head and raised her hands in submission. The woman began laughing.

"Oh no, it's too late for all that now after how annoying you've been," she laughed.

She put the gun under Kim's chin and lifted it, forcing her to look directly into her eyes. Kim quickly shut her eyes and turned her head to the side. The woman took a blade in her other hand and raised it to Kim's cheek, she gently turned her head back so that she was facing her. She leaned in close as she spoke to her.

"I respect your skill, you've obviously got some training behind you, but you're jumping into things a lot bigger than yourself.... whoever you are."

Kim opened her eyes and shot her a hateful gaze. She seemed taken aback by this. She leaned back a bit looking Kim up and down. Her stare was no longer arrogant, but curious. She seemed almost intimidated even.

She stabbed the blade into the ground behind her out of Kim's reach and held the gun up to the side of her head. With the other hand she reached for the scarf covering Kim's mouth. Kim was shocked, her heart began racing as the woman began pulling the scarf from over her mouth and head. Kim pulled back away from her.

"Hey, be still!" she commanded, continuing to unwrap the scarf.

Kim noticed her tone had changed as well. She sounded concerned. She removed the scarf and Kim immediately fell back into a bow, closing her eyes. She pulled the blade from the ground and put it up to Kim's neck. She again put the gun under Kim's chin and raised it forcing Kim to face her.

"Open your eyes," she told her.

Kim refused, keeping them shut as she turned away.

"Open your eyes!" she demanded, shaking Kim hard.

She firmly pressed the blade against Kim's exposed neck and rammed the gun hard into the side of her head. Kim opened her eyes focusing hard on her. The woman's breaths grew short and her eyes had again begun to read something different, this time fear.

"No..." the woman faintly whispered.

Kim watched as she fell deeper into what seemed like panic. She was shaking, breathing harder, gasping for air. She stuck the blade back into the ground behind her and placed her hand gently on Kim's shoulder. She continued to study her harder and harder. They made eye contact and the woman spoke.

".... Kim?" she asked in a cracking voice.

Kim jerked back a bit, surprised by the speaking of her name. The woman shut her eyes and turned her head away in disgust.

"Oh my god, no, no way…" she whispered aloud.

There was a tremble in her voice as she spoke. She turned back and reached for Kim's chest. She grabbed her gold chain and pulled it out from under her shirt. She held the chain with the charm resting across her fingertips. Kim quickly glanced down at the chain and back up at her. Kim could see the sadness in her eyes, something had triggered her.

The woman suddenly fell back away from her, dropping the gun at her side. Her breaths were rapid and heavy as though she were hyperventilating. Kim dropped her hands puzzled by her sudden panic.

"Do I know you?" Kim asked.

Still struggling to breathe, she couldn't answer her.

"Are you OK?" Kim asked.

She was still unable to answer as she continued fighting to find air. Kim rose to her feet and walked over to her. She stopped just inches away, looked down at her, and eventually extended her hand out. The woman's eyes lit up as she stared up at Kim obviously doubtful. Kim extended her hand out further assuring her she no longer meant any harm to her. She reached out, grabbed Kim's hand, and was pulled to her feet.

Once standing, the woman backed away from her. Her breaths slowing down, becoming more controlled.

"Are you OK?" Kim asked again.

The woman reached into one of the pouches on the waist pack at her side. Kim braced herself to dodge another blade but she instead pulled out a small square piece of paper. She began slowly stepping towards Kim.

"How do you know my name, have we met?" Kim asked.

"Y-yes, but you wouldn't remember me," she said.

She stopped a few feet from Kim and removed her hood and mask revealing her face. Kim immediately noticed her features; they looked familiar.

"Kim.... I'm your sister," she said.

Kim looked at her puzzled, feeling almost insulted by her claim.

"Ummm…. no, sorry," Kim shook her head, "you must have me confused with someone else, I'm an only child."

The woman extended the piece of paper she was holding out to her. She nodded, beckoning Kim to take it. Kim took it from her and saw that it was actually an old polaroid photograph. Her heart immediately plunged into her stomach. The photo was identical to the damaged one she had of her parents on her refrigerator, but it was complete. No burned edges cutting off her parent's heads.

She saw herself in her mother's arms and the portion of the photo she had never been able to see; her mother and father's faces, and in her father's arms, another child that looked identical to her.

The woman reached over and pointed to Kim in the photo, "…. that's you."

Kim looked up at her, she looked as though she were about to burst into tears.

"Kim.... we thought…. we thought you were dead."

Chapter 5

Merry Christmas

"I know I know.... I'm sorry, something came up and I just had to go. I promise I'll explain everything as soon as I can," Kim said into her phone.

LuLu was on the other end. She wasn't happy upon finding out that Kim had ditched her and Cindy at the banquet hall. She was demanding an explanation.

"No no, it's not that I promise. Look, I know you hate me right now but I really have to go. Please, just take Cindy home for me. I'll explain it all in the morning OK?" she said.

The sound of the phone hanging up without a proper goodbye from LuLu made Kim feel awful. She knew she was upset, but she also believed she would understand once she had a chance to explain the situation to her.

Kim was sitting on a bar stool inside a late night diner, waiting. She shoved her phone down into her pocket and began gently massaging the sides of her head. It was pounding, a thousand thoughts raced through it every passing second. She felt like her head was going to explode. Her hand still stung from the blade that had hit it and her ribs had also began aching again from the kick she had taken to them.

"Long night?"

Kim looked up and saw Helena standing behind the counter gently smiling at her.

"Not tonight Helena, please..." she sighed, dropping her head back down.

Helena shrugged and quietly stepped away.

"Here you go Kim," a man said as he pushed through the kitchen door holding two mugs in his hand.

He had a bushy red mustache that sat above a friendly grin.

"Thanks Paul," she said softly, taking the mugs from him.

"You OK?" the man asked, "You look beat."

Kim looked at him and shook her head.

"If I told you just half the story you wouldn't believe it," she breathed.

The man chuckled and patted Kim on her shoulder.

"Take care kid, Merry Christmas," he said before disappearing back into the kitchen.

"You too," she replied.

She turned around holding a mug in each hand and made her way to the small booth where the woman she had fought in the alley was sitting. She placed one mug in front of her, keeping hold of the other.

She sat down and looked her over from across

the tabletop. Now under the lighting of the diner Kim saw that she couldn't deny her. Their resemblance was uncanny, they weren't just sisters, they were twins. She looked to be a bit smaller in both size and stature than she was, which made Kim even more surprised by the fight she put up against her. Her hair was black as opposed to Kim's brown and much longer, stopping a little below shoulder length with a few bangs hanging in front of her face. They both shared the same brown eyes and skin color, although she had a few freckles scattered about her cheeks that Kim didn't.

For Kim, it was almost scary looking at her. Aside from their different hair styling and color, they were spitting images of each other.

"Thanks," she whispered, "how much do I owe you?"

"It's on the house," Kim said, "I know the owner. My friends and I use to play at the basketball courts across the street and then come in here and spend all our money. We practically kept this place in business back then."

"I'm surprised it's even open, Christmas is like an hour away."

"They don't close, they honestly can't afford to. It's a family owned place and lucky for them they're a big family, so they rotate shifts as needed. Open twenty-four hours a day all year long," Kim explained.

"I see," she nodded.

A brief silence came between them that Kim eventually broke.

"So, Rin…. how's your arm?" Kim asked.

She had wrapped her arm with a piece of the scarf Kim had had wrapped over her head.

"It's seen better days, but the bleedings stopped, it's fine. How's your hand?"

"It's been through worse." she said, flexing it a bit, "That kick to the ribs is what might do me in though."

"Sorry," she shrugged.

Kim shrugged herself and took a sip of her tea; Rin did the same. Kim noticed a horrified look come over her face as she spit the tea back into the mug.

"Y-you OK?" she asked.

"This tea is ice cold..." she said.

"Oh…. yeah that's how I drink mine..."

Rin flashed her a look of disgust, as if she had never heard of such a thing.

"Ummm…. I'm sorry. Here, I can get him to heat it up..." Kim reached out to grab the mug.

"It's fine, don't worry about it…." she pushed the mug aside.

Rin began scratching her head, thinking.

"I…. uhhh…. do you know what happened…. all those years ago?" she asked.

The look on her face told she was almost afraid of what Kim's answer might be. Kim set her mug down and pushed it aside.

"I was gonna ask you the same thing," she shrugged.

Rin fell back into the booth seat and took a moment to collect her thoughts. Kim noticed she was wearing a gold chain identical to her own. Just like hers, it had a small charm on it that read her name in a cursive font.

"I-I don't even know where to start cause.... well.... I don't know what you know," she said.

"Just start somewhere. Tell me what you know, I'll tell you what I know, and we'll just try to fill in the blanks as best we can," Kim said.

"OK.... well, the Joy City raids. You live here, I assume you've heard of them right?"

"Of course."

"Well, that's where it all started I guess. Some years ago, when we would've just been babies, some gang, I forget the name of them..."

"The Colt 45s," Kim said.

".... yeah, I think that was them, that kinda rings a bell," she said.

She seemed surprised Kim knew the name so quickly; Kim was surprised she didn't.

"Anyway, a long time ago they raided the city and it was bad, really bad, like the city was literally in flames. The little neighborhood we lived in got burned to the ground. People started to evacuate, the city became a dead zone almost overnight. They said there was no way to help it, no way to save it. So they decided to just let it rot from the inside. Anyone who was bold enough to stay was considered suicidal, and no neighboring city or county or anything wanted to lend the resources to help, they just gave up on it. It was complete and utter chaos. So of course, having a pair of newborn twins, Mom and Dad decided to leave, go east and get as far away from here as possible. Well, the day they decided to evacuate..."

She swallowed heavily breaking her sentence.

".... they never told me exactly what happened, but..."

Rin paused again choking up a bit. Kim was staring impatiently, waiting for her to continue.

".... I mean, remember, the entire city was seeing red, there was no police force, nothing was being regulated, the law was dead in the area, the city was in complete turmoil. To this day I still don't know everything because they just refused to ever tell me, and I believe it was partially due to them feeling so guilty about it, so upset with themselves over what happened that day, but somehow.... they lost you."

Kim's mouth fell open.

"I don't know how or where but somehow they looked up and you just weren't there. The only thing I was ever able to get out of them was that they had us wrapped in blankets, inside shopping carts or something and there were just so many people running and screaming in the streets, it was so chaotic. They looked up and you were just gone. Once they realized you weren't there, they canceled their leave and stayed months searching everywhere for you, but they got the same answer everywhere they went. Anyone lost was considered a fatality, no survivors, young or old."

As Kim listened she read the sorrow on Rin's face. She was in an immense amount of emotional distress just speaking of the happening, yet she herself would've been too young at the time to have actually remembered it.

"I don't wanna say they gave up, but they were

heartbroken and scared and Joy City just wasn't..."

"Wasn't helping," Kim finished her sentence, "not much has changed since then, crime still goes unpunished every day, reports go uninvestigated, and this city gets darker and darker every day. You can get away with anything here. I can only imagine how bad it was with the entire city in a state of emergency."

"They couldn't find you, it was impossible. Police stations, hospitals, shelters, they were all shut down. So, we moved east and I guess they just tried to start over. I'm sorry, had they known, I know they wouldn't have..."

"It's fine, I know how this place is. They, along with the rest of the people in the city, had to be going through hell on earth during all that."

"Yeah, so.... is all this news to you or.... well, I guess not, you knew the gang's name..."

"Believe it or not, that gang still exists in the city today and me and them have become very familiar as of recently, so yes, I do know of them, what they did, and the role they played in my life, or *our* lives, I guess. Of course, I don't remember anything about the raids either, but living here as long as I have I've heard about them a lot. No one was ever super clear with me about what happened, but I guess after I was lost.... someone found me and I ended up in the foster care system. I bounced around from place to place for a while and by the time I got somewhere and stuck, and was old enough to where they felt like they could tell me something, there were so many different stories being told to me,

I was left more confused than anything else about where I came from."

Rin looked at her through teary eyes. Kim could see her trying to empathize with the pain and uncertainty Kim had dealt with growing up.

"I'm sorry you had to go through that. I can't even imagine having to wonder where your parents and sister were for all this time…"

"*Sister?*" Kim shook her head, "Everyone comes from a set of parents so I knew I had at least that somewhere out in the world, but I was completely unaware you even existed until about an hour ago."

Rin was surprised to hear this. She pulled the photo of them and their parents from her pocket and laid it down on the table. After only being able to see the small portion of the photo she could for twenty-six years it was surreal to her to actually see the whole thing. She couldn't believe how much she looked like her mother. Rin placed a finger on the photo.

"This was tucked into the frame of one of my school pictures we had hanging up in the house for years. I would always pass by it and wonder who you were, but it was years before I ever actually asked about you. When I finally did and they told me about you and what happened, I think I was about six maybe.... I didn't really have a reaction at first. It was weird to think about but I just didn't really pay it any mind initially. But once I got into my teens, I don't know why but my curiosity just randomly piqued and I was suddenly so interested in this sister that I knew nothing about, so I asked them about you again. They must've had a million stories about you, about us. It made me realize how hurt they must've been losing you, how much they missed you. It also made me realize why they were so protective of me growing up."

Kim could feel herself getting choked up. Her eyes were tearing up, her palms were sweating, she bit her lower lip to hide it quivering.

"They talked about me?" she asked softly.

"All the time." Rin smiled, "That one day I asked about you spawned countless more after where they'd actually come and sit me down to talk about you. They told me so much, I mean everything. Even though I couldn't remember you, I felt like I knew you just from all the stories they had about us as babies. Just the short time that you were with us, it seemed like they had a story to tell for every minute of every day."

Kim smiled faintly. She couldn't believe what she was hearing but she was falling in love with every word. She looked at Rin smiling herself as she continued pulling from her memories.

"They always use to talk about your eyes. They said there was only one other person on this planet with eyes as big and brown as mine, that's how I recognized you so quickly back there."

Kim suddenly took notice to how big Rin's eyes were. Just like her own. Suddenly Rin's smile faded, her disposition dipped, and her voice got weak.

"But then dementia hit them both. Early Onset

Alzheimer's actually. Somedays they'd forget they had another daughter, somedays they'd forget they had kids at all. Then both their health started failing, and I just didn't wanna upset them and risk anything happening.... so I stopped asking about you and then..."

She seemed to lose herself in her thoughts, staring into space for a moment. Kim leaned in a little closer grabbing her attention again.

".... sorry." Rin continued, "I use to just stare at this picture every day for hours just wondering what you would've been like, what it would've been like to have a sister..."

Kim ran her finger gently over the photo.

"I.... I used to stare at the same picture, wondering what mom and dad would've been like.... I didn't even know about you, but.... I just wish I could've met them before..." Kim trailed off into silence.

Rin raised her head slowly making eye contact with her. She waited for Kim to finish but she dropped her head unable to keep speaking.

"Before what?" Rin asked.

"Before.... you know..." Kim lost her words again.

Rin continued to stare at her puzzled.

"I don't know what you mean..." she said.

".... never mind." Kim said, changing the subject, "So what brought you to Joy City? And why were you after that guy?"

Rin looked reluctant to speak. A look of shame washed over her as she gathered her words.

"Well, we needed money fast, we were running out of options. Mom and Dad had gotten too sick to take care of themselves, so I dropped out of school and moved back in to take care of them because I didn't want them to end up in a retirement home or anything like that. But I was in way over my head. I had student loans to pay, their medical bills, my car note, the house note, I just couldn't handle it all on the little paycheck I got from clearing off tables, and so someone..."

"Wait..." Kim interrupted her, "Mom and Dad?"

".... yeah?"

"Wait, when is all of this happening?" Kim asked.

"What do you mean?"

"You moving in to take care of Mom and Dad?"

"I don't know, maybe like six months ago?" she shrugged.

"But you said *we* needed money?"

"We did? I mean we still do but..."

"Who's we?"

Rin looked her over as if she were insane.

"Me, Mom, and Dad?"

"Mom and Dad?! They're alive?!" Kim asked, her voice echoed inside the empty diner.

She had stood completely out of her seat and was leaning over the tabletop. Rin had leaned back into her seat a bit startled by Kim suddenly springing up.

"What? Who said they weren't?"

"You said their health had been failing and..."

"It.... it is? Wait, is that what you meant by you wish you'd met them before?"

"I-I thought you meant..." Kim froze.

Her heart started pounding, she couldn't breathe, she felt dizzy and off balance. Rin was still staring at her from her sudden irruption.

"Kim," she grabbed her by her shoulders and forced her back down, "calm down before you pass out."

Kim struggled to catch her breath, gasping for air.

"Wow, we really are twins, panic attacks not even an hour apart," Rin grinned.

"Where.... where are they?" Kim breathed.

"That retirement home down on uhhh.... Minneola I think is the name of the street? Greentree, the place is called. Normally they don't accept temporary stays but I had a friend back home call in a favor for me. I really really didn't wanna bring them back here with all the bad memories they probably have associated with this place but they're way too sick to leave alone and..."

"*Greentree?!* They're in Joy City?!" she sprung up from her seat again.

Rin jumped at her voice echoing off the walls as she stood hovering over the tabletop again.

"Kim, sit down, and stop yelling.... I know it's just us in here, but..."

"Take me to see them!" she demanded.

"What?"

"I need to see them now!"

"Kim, it's past ten. Visiting hours are over, we can go see them tomorrow..."

"No! We're.... *I'm* going now!" she said, sliding out the booth.

"What.... Kim?!" Rin slid out behind her.

Kim dropped a ten-dollar bill on the table and darted for the door.

"Kim, they're not gonna let you in," Rin said.

"They will if I tell them it's an emergency," she insisted.

She stepped outside and began marching down the sidewalk. Rin ran right behind her and placed her hand on her shoulder spinning her around.

"Kim wait..."

"Look," she barked back, "my entire life all I had was half a photo and a necklace. You just told me their health is poor, I gotta make every second count, I'm going to see them now."

Rin could feel the rigor in her voice. She wasn't asking, she was telling. She surrendered, removing her hand from her shoulder.

"Alright," she shrugged, "well let's at least call a cab."

~

After a short drive they arrived to a mostly empty parking lot.

Only about three vehicles sat outside under a glowing green sign that read "Greentree Senior and Retirement Homes".

"Thank you so much," Kim said, handing the

driver a wad of cash before quickly hopping out the cab.

Rin's mouth fell open noticing that she had given the driver way too much money.

"My pleasure ladies.... Merry Christmas?" the man stuttered as he stared at the cash in awe.

Rin shook her head and quietly scoffed as she exited the car. Kim started speed walking towards the building. There looked to be a single light on from what she could see from the double doors leading inside. Rin stepped in front of Kim and grabbed her shoulder.

"Hey, I wouldn't get too excited, they're not gonna let us in. It's way past visiting hours," Rin warned.

"Yes they will," Kim said, pushing her aside.

"Well you're definitely your mother's daughter, just as stubborn as her," Rin mumbled, following behind her.

They came up to the door and peeked through the glass. They saw only one person inside standing behind the front desk. A petite red headed girl in a pair of thick black framed glasses lost in her phone.

"Oh, it's Sydney," Rin said.

"You know her?"

"I mean, not really, but she was here when I dropped them off here last week. Super sweet girl, we might've lucked out."

Kim pulled open the door and stepped inside. The girl immediately placed her phone down, and looked up adjusting her glasses.

"Ummm.... how can I help..." she began.

She looked past Kim and made eye contact with Rin.

"Oh hey.... ummm.... Rin right?" she asked.

Rin stepped in front of Kim.

"Yes, I brought my parents in about a week ago."

"Yeah yeah, I remember. Ummm…. how can I help you?" she asked.

"Ummm.... so I know it's super late and normally you probably wouldn't be able to do this, but is there any way you could let us back to see my parents.... *our* parents? This is my sister," she said pointing to Kim.

"Ummm.... visiting hours are actually over, but you can come back at seven a.m. and stay all day until ten. It'll be pretty busy with it being Christmas and all, but you're welcome to drop by and…"

"Listen Sydney, I know it's a kind of strange request but we really need to see them now. My sister, it's a long story but she's never met them before, and she just really needs to see them, just for a second."

The girl looked back and forth between the two of them for a moment but eventually stood back on her original statement.

"I'm sorry. If I could, I would, but I'm not allowed to let anyone back outside of visiting hours," she said shrugging.

Rin nodded and turned to Kim.

"We'll come back as soon..."

Kim pushed her aside and leaned over the counter top.

"Please, you don't understand, I need to see my parents. Their health's not that good right now, please, every second counts, please?" she begged.

The girl again looked back and forth between the two of them.

"Just give us five minutes, please, she really needs this. Five minutes and we'll be out the door I promise," Rin pleaded.

Sydney scratched her head and bit her lip thinking for a moment.

"Uhhh.... five minutes?"

"She just wants to see them," Rin said.

After thinking it over for another moment, she caved looking at the hopeless pout on Kim's face. She nodded her head standing from her chair.

"OK listen," she whispered to them, "I'm not supposed to do this. I can give you five minutes to see them but then I gotta get you outta here before anyone sees you, OK?"

"Thank you, thank you so much," Rin said.

"C'mon, but we gotta be quiet," she whispered.

They both nodded. They followed her through a door and down a wide cream colored hallway. The walls were lined on both sides with flowers and paintings of sunsets and meadows. A golden plaque was attached to the front of each door reading either a name or two and a number.

She took a left as the hallway split and walked down to the very end where she stopped and stood in front of a door on the right side. On the door in place of the golden plaque the others had was a white piece of paper taped down. Written in black marker Kim read the names and number on the paper silently to herself.

"1018 Ben & Sue"

Her heart pounding, beating faster and faster every second. It felt as if it were going to burst right out of her chest. Her palms got sweaty and she grew short of breath.

"Five minutes OK? You normally wouldn't wanna wake anyone their ages with dementia up cold but we'll give it a try," Sydney said.

She pulled a key ring from her waist and began searching for the correct one. Rin pulled Kim back by the arm and turned her around to face her.

"Before you see them, I just wanna prepare you. Their dementia's gotten really bad, both of them. I just don't want you to be upset if they don't remember you. Like I said, sometimes they don't even remember me."

Kim couldn't respond; the moment had already rendered her entirely numb. Sydney found the key and stuck it into the door. She turned it and pulled the door open just a crack. The faint hum of a voice speaking poured out. Sydney and Rin looked at each other puzzled.

"Is that them?" Rin asked.

"They wouldn't still be up this late would they?" Sydney asked looking at Rin.

Before she could answer Kim pushed Sydney out the way, grabbed the door, and swung it open just wide enough for her to squeeze through.

"Wh-Kim wait!" Rin whispered.

Both Rin and Sydney rushed inside after her.

They almost ran her over upon entering as she had stopped just a few feet from the doorway. She was frozen, looking forward with the blankest of stares on her face. Just a few feet from her sat two people sitting in rocking chairs side by side staring back at her. An elderly woman and man, who even in their old age she could tell shared her features.

The woman had her eyes, the color specifically, the part of her hair that wasn't grey matched the color of her own, and even amongst the many wrinkles in her face a resemblance could easily be found.

The man's thin lips, the cut of his eyes, his nose; it was an unmistakable match. Even though he was seated she could tell from looking at his legs he was tall like her.

All five were mute, stuck waiting for one of the others to speak and break the silence. The only sound in the room was the light hum of the voices coming from the TV. Rin stepped forward and knelt down next to the old man's chair.

"Hey, what are you guys still doing up? Are you OK?" she asked him.

He didn't answer as his focus was locked on Kim. Rin moved around him and squatted next to the woman's chair.

"Hey, you guys were in bed when I left, what happened?" she asked.

The woman didn't answer either as she too was laser focused on Kim. Rin looked back and saw a look on Kim's face she couldn't recall having ever seen on anyone before in her life. It was both blank yet full of emotion. Now crouched in between them both, she placed hands on both the man and woman's arms. In unison they both turned towards her. She looked them both in the eyes and then looked back towards Kim.

"Mom.... Dad..." Rin began with a deep sigh, "listen, I need you both to try as hard as you can to remember right now. This is gonna be impossible to explain right now, but this.... this is...."

"Kim," the woman said softly.

Every eye in the room immediately locked on her. Rin looked at her with her mouth nearly on the floor. She glanced back at Kim for a quick moment and saw she herself was awestruck.

"You.... you remember her?" Rin whimpered.

"Of course I do, she's my daughter," she said with a slight smile.

"Kim..." the man repeated with a small smile of his own.

Kim began to slowly approach them, taking one small step every second or two until she was within just inches of where they sat. She dropped to her knees and looked back and forth between the two of them. She looked at Rin crouched in between them and saw herself, saw her twin sister, and had to blink a few times to remind herself she wasn't dreaming, this was really happening.

She placed one hand on the man's hand and the other on the woman's. The feel of their skin against her own felt surreal. Upon touching them she immediately felt a spark, something she had never felt before in her life. And at that moment she knew without a doubt who the two sitting in front of her were. She bowed her head, and began to cry.

"Mom.... Dad..." she sobbed.

Her mother placed a hand on her back.

"We missed you darling," she said softly.

"This is…. this is my daughter," the man proudly announced, smiling to Sydney still standing by the doorway.

Rin fell back onto her hands, closed her eyes, and released a heavy sigh as she began to smile. She was beyond exhausted but the scene in front of her brought an indescribable amount of joy and relief.

"What a night..." she whispered to herself grinning.

She looked up and saw Kim sobbing on her knees as their parents comforted her with warm smiles and loving words.

Sydney standing at the door silently mouthed to Rin, "Ten more minutes."

Rin mouthed a thank you back to her for the extra time and understanding. She slipped out into the hallway, gently closing the door behind her.

Rin continued smiling as she watched the three of them. She couldn't remember a time seeing her parents so happy, so lively, especially in their old age. Her smile grew bigger and bigger every second that went by. She glanced up at a clock hanging on the wall.

"12:04" it read

"Merry Christmas guys," she said to the three of them.

Chapter 6

The Fall

Kim stood in her kitchen leaning against the counter top with a wad of tissues clutched in her hand. Her cheeks stained with dried tears. Her eyes were heavy, she was exhausted. The last time she remembered crying so hard for so long was the day she was told about the murder of her foster parents. It was such a familiar sob, so uncontrollable that submitting to it seemed like the only way to have it pass, yet the feeling, the reason for the tears were so different.

She wiped her eyes a few more times taking several long deep breaths.

"Kim..."

She turned and saw Helena leaning up against the counter next to her. Of course, a smile on her face.

".... how do you feel?"

She sucked in some air and exhaled from her mouth before speaking.

"I-I mean obviously, I'm happy..." she said, her voice cracking with every word, ".... but..."

"Don't explain, that's all that matters," Helena whispered back.

She had a response but went mute as Rin returned from the bathroom.

"You're running low on hand soap sis, I'd..." she paused as she saw Kim's face, "You're still crying? You big baby."

Kim rolled her eyes at her tease. She dropped her tissues in the trashcan and picked up two glasses of tea from the counter. She sat down and slid one across the table to Rin.

"Nice place you got here," Rin said, taking a sip.

"Yeah, I uhhh…. was able to..." Kim paused as Rin's face molded into a horrible frown.

"What's wrong?" Kim asked.

"You and this cold tea. Whoever put you on that didn't love you," Rin cried pushing the glass to the center of the table.

Kim cut her eyes to Helena as she rounded the corner into the living room with a smile.

"Anyway," Kim began, "this has been one of the craziest nights of my life but I just wanna say thank you. You have no idea what meeting them tonight meant to me. I've spent my whole life wondering you know, and to actually finally meet them…. and you..."

"Hey, thank *you*." Rin returned, "I've lived with them nearly all twenty-six years of my life. Never have I seen their eyes light up more than the moment they saw you, can't remember the last time I saw them that happy period. I'm glad we found each other, and I'm glad you got to meet them."

They both shared a smile.

"Although, I am a little jealous mom recognized you as quickly as she did when she can barely remember my name most days," Rin laughed.

"Yeah, that was a surprise to me too." Kim said, "Hey, how old are they?"

"Dad's fifty-nine, Mom's fifty-seven," she said. "That's it?"

"Yeah, I know, they look way older huh?"

"You'd think seventies just looking at them but they got kids in their mid-twenties," Kim added.

"A combination of stress, pain, and just not taking care of themselves. After what happened with you way back then, a lot of the family kind of turned their backs on them for some reason. That hurt them a lot. Then we moved out east and we never really saw or heard from any of them ever again. Because of that, they spoiled me rotten, did everything for me, always made sure I was taken care of and then some, as any good parents would. But too often, they overextended themselves and in doing that, they neglected their own health. I didn't realize it until I'd moved out but I ended up moving right back in not too long after once they got too sick to take care of themselves."

She grew quiet for a moment searching for the next thing to say. She placed her hand under her chin and looked down at her reflection in the glass tabletop.

"I hate that that was your real first image of them. They've looked better but also much worse believe it or not. Anyway, I had a job bussing tables but it just wasn't enough to keep the lights on, keep the water running, and pay their medical bills and all that, and so to make ends meet.... that's when I started to..."

She looked at Kim assuming she knew what she was getting at.

"Ummm.... yeah, let's talk about that cause..." Kim stopped as she heard Cindy's door open from upstairs.

"Mom?!" she shouted from the top of the stairs.

Kim groaned as she was instantly pulled from her night of surprises back to where it all began, ditching her daughter and friend at a Christmas banquet. She looked up at Rin to find her smiling ear to ear.

"Mom?" Rin asked delighted, "I'm an Aunt?"

"I'm down here Cin, come here!" Kim shouted.

Her steps were heavy, Kim knew why. She made it to the bottom and twisted her face at Kim.

"Thanks for ditchin us at..." she stopped once she saw Rin smiling at her.

She quickly glanced at Kim and then back to Rin.

"Oh, hello," Cindy said timidly.

"Hi," Rin cheerfully grinned.

Cindy quickly scooted past her and stood next to Kim. She watched Rin cautiously never taking her eyes off her.

"Kim, aren't you gonna introduce us?" Rin asked.

Kim looked at her with tired eyes from behind her glass of tea.

"Do I have to?"

Rin sucked her teeth at her.

"Alright alright. Cin listen," she began, "to say the least this has been one of the wildest nights of my life and it's mostly thanks to this woman right here. It's way too complicated to explain at the moment but this is my sister Rin, your new Auntie."

Cindy looked Rin up and down puzzled.

"*Sister?*" she repeated.

"*Twin* sister," Rin politely corrected her.

Cindy looked back and forth between the two of them a few times then her face suddenly lit up.

"Whoa, y'all *are* twins, like real twins.... wait, when'd you get a sister?" she asked Kim.

"About twenty-six years ago I guess. Trust me, I'm just as shocked as you are, but Merry Christmas, she's your present," Kim said, taking a sip of her tea.

"So, were you two like separated at birth or something? How'd you find out about each other?" she asked.

Rin's smile disappeared immediately; she began stumbling over her words.

"Ummm.... we ummm.... we.... we met at your mom's job," she said.

"Job? She doesn't have a job," Cindy said.

Kim snickered a bit behind her glass, "Smooth sis, you really sold that one."

"I uhhh..." Rin searched for an escape.

"It's OK, Rin. She knows," Kim said, standing from the table.

"She knows?" Rin asked.

"I'm not proud of it but the kid's sharp, she figured it out before I said a word to her," Kim explained walking her glass over to the sink.

"Oh.... OK.... well uhhh..."

".... yeah?" Cindy asked still waiting for an answer.

Kim looked over her shoulder and shook her head at Rin.

"It's fine Rin," Kim assured her again, "we were after the same person Cin. We threw some knives at each other, punched each other in the face a few times, I cut her arm, she kicked me in my ribs, then we realized we were related and made up. Normal sister stuff."

"Really?" Cindy laughed, "Fun night you two had I guess."

Rin's eyes had grown huge. She was a bit thrown by how casual Kim and Cindy were with the subject.

"Ummm.... yeah, it was a night alright," she said under her breath.

"Wait, that's crazy. So, you're twins and both ended up being assassins?"

"Well actually I'm not an assassin. I'm more of a mercenary," Rin corrected her.

"What's the difference?" Cindy asked.

"As a mercenary, I work for anyone who pays me and whoever pays the most. Assassins usually work in guilds or within a team. I don't actually work with anyone."

"Hmph.... I see."

"Cin stop hounding her, she's obviously uncomfortable talking about it," Kim said as she began washing out her glass.

"OK OK, at least tell me this, who's older?" Cindy asked.

Kim paused and turned her head around a bit interested in the answer herself. She realized the topic hadn't yet come up. Rin smiled a little before answering noticing her sudden intrigue.

"Your mom is my older sister, she beat me by about six minutes."

Kim silently turned her head back around and continued washing out her glass.

"Hmmm..." Cindy thought for a moment searching for another question, "What are your parents like?"

"Cin, enough," Kim said.

Kim had cried enough already; the last thing she needed was a recap of what she had seen for herself.

"I'll tell you about them later OK?" Rin promised her.

"When's later? How long are you gonna be in town? Do you live here?"

"Cindy?!" Kim roared again, "Quit it?!"

"Kim, she's fine, really. I live on the east coast. I don't really know how long I'll be out here to be honest. I came out here for.... work.... and at the moment I'm not really sure I'm gonna be able to complete it so I don't actually know how long I'll be out this way."

"You didn't complete it Sunday?" Kim asked.

"What do you mean?"

"Sunday, that was you on the yacht wasn't it, that took out that guy and cleaned out his safe?"

"Oh yeah.... wait, you were there?"

"I walked in a few minutes after you left out the window. I was supposed to be getting whatever was in that safe," Kim explained.

"Oh, well, there was only like two grand in cash in it, definitely not what my source told me I'd find, and I doubt it's what you would've been expecting either."

"Definitely not," Kim confirmed.

"I mean, I'll split my cut of it with you if you want?" Rin offered.

"Keep it, use it to take care of Mom and Dad."

Rin nodded.

"Anyway, my source confirmed that that guy was just a front man anyway. The guy with the real money was the one you've been guarding me from these past few days. Did you say you were after him too, cause it hasn't really seemed like it?"

"Yeah, about that. I was on him for about an hour, and then he managed to say all the right things and I just couldn't do it. The guy and his wife are adopting a little girl from the same foster home I spent most of my childhood in. It's also where I adopted Cindy from. I was in the same position that little girl is in right now about twenty or so years ago, and I know exactly what's going through her head right now. When a child ends up in a foster home, nine times outta ten they're feeling unwanted, thrown away even. Finally, someone comes along and wants them. I couldn't take that away from her, and once I decided I wasn't gonna kill him myself, I wasn't gonna let you do it either."

"I see," Rin nodded.

"I'm sorry if that makes your trip out here an empty one but we'll talk. Whatever you were gonna get for it, I'll give it to you."

"How?" she asked.

"Don't worry about it, we'll talk."

"Alright," Rin nodded.

"It's interesting that those two were connected though, I wasn't aware of that."

Kim tried to recall any clues that could've possibly linked the men but she couldn't piece anything together.

"I just chalked it up as Joy City. I have literally no memories of this place being here only as a baby, but I've heard just about every story that's been told about it. People say it's just normal for people to do bad out here, it's what keeps the city going."

"Unfortunately. So what made you start doing what you're doing, just money?" Kim asked.

"Pretty much. I'm up to my neck in debt and there was just no way we were gonna be able to make it much longer without some extra cash. I started selling drugs here and there off the streets but that didn't last long cause I didn't know the first thing about what I was selling or how much I should've been selling it for. So I went back to the guy I was getting them from and told him I really needed help making some kind of sustainable cash fast and he told me he had a job he'd pay me five grand for."

Rin paused and shivered in disgust.

"I shot and killed a man that night." she said, obviously ashamed of her actions, "I know it was wrong but we needed the money so bad…"

"You don't have to justify yourself to me. If I had a body count as low as yours I might actually still have a shot at makin it to heaven. You're fine. Worse thing you did was take five grand for a kill, if it was less than a twenty-four hour notice he owed you at least twenty."

Rin shrugged.

"He introduced me to some guys that taught me how to fight, how to use a gun and knife, and then after one or two more kills he suggested making a trip out here if I really wanted to make some money. Said he knew of a couple people out here with tickets already on their heads."

"From all the way out on the east coast? That's odd," Kim said, crossing her arms.

"I don't know, he travels a lot. I'm sure he has his hands in all kinds of dirt in a bunch of different places. But anyway, I really didn't wanna come here because I knew what memories this city held for them you know. But with what I was planning on doing, I kept hearing 'go to Joy City, you can get away with anything there, people make bank knockin people off over there.' I didn't want to but we weren't gonna be able to survive much longer. I didn't feel like I had a choice."

"Mom and Dad don't know that you're…"

"No, of course not. I couldn't tell them that. I told them this was a business trip, and whether they believed me or just didn't care to challenge, they went along with it. Unfortunately, when we moved east none of the family came with us so I didn't have anyone to leave them with. So, I had to bring them out here with me. Putting them on that plane was terrifying."

"Do they know where they are?"

"No, I doubt they recognize it at all after twenty plus years. They didn't ask either so I didn't bother telling them. To be honest, my plan was to come, make a little money, and then leave as soon as possible. Just in case it did eventually click or they heard something. The thing is though, considering what I'm doing, and how much people who do it out here make doing it, it doesn't really make sense to leave. I was surprised to find there were so many people who actually do it out here, almost like a profession. Like there's actually teams in this city that do just that."

"Team..." Kim corrected her.

"What?"

"A team, not teams. There's just one out here and it's us. We call it The Pool. We take a lot of contracts annually and we've been doing it for years. It may look like a bunch of teams out here but it's really just us, a team of five. We make sure of that."

"How'd you fall into somethin like that?"

"My foster parents actually, but that's a whole 'nother long sad story. I'll tell you about it another time."

Rin began thinking then suddenly her stare went blank.

"The Pool?" Rin asked.

"Yeah, it's just a name it took on. We work out of an abandoned pool hall."

Rin's eyes grew wide as she started to stare into space. Kim and Cindy both caught her zoning out and traded confused looks.

"Hey," Kim snapped her fingers in front of her face, "what's up, you OK?"

She came to and looked at Kim horrified.

"Where's this pool hall at?" Rin asked.

"Basically nowhere, I mean it's not even on most Joy City maps. It's tucked off in the woods somewhere, like I said it's abandoned."

".... oh god," Rin shivered.

She placed her hand up to her mouth and stared at Kim in horror. Kim stared back puzzled.

"What?" she asked.

"I think.... I-I think I messed up Kim..."

"Messed up?"

Kim and Cindy traded stares. Rin was shaking, stuttering over her words as she spoke.

"W-when I came here, I knew th-that there were already groups in the city making money off killing people. He…. he told me to really make money out here I'd need to get rid of them first..."

"*He?* He who? Get rid of who? What are you talking about?"

Rin clinched her teeth and winced.

"Earlier tonight, before I came to the banquet hall, I-I went back to the same bar we ran into each other at the night before looking for that man…. and I-I saw two women and a man camped out on the rooftops. They looked like they were waiting for someone, I assumed the same guy. Eventually the man with them took off and left. I followed him, he went into this small run down building that looked like it hadn't been occupied in years and..." her words tapered off into silence.

"Rin..."

"I-I was thinking I needed to get rid of them.... so, I-I called..."

"Rin you didn't?" Kim gasped.

"I-I'm sorry," she cried, "maybe they didn't take it seriously. Isn't Joy City's police notorious for letting stuff go unchecked?"

Kim looked at her through heartbroken eyes. While she knew Rin couldn't have known, she couldn't help but feel betrayed.

"Oh my god..." Kim grumbled.

She ran past Rin and rocketed up the stairs. She burst through her bedroom door and pulled open one of the drawers on her nightstand. She reached in and pulled out a burner phone.

She unlocked it and saw, "5 missed calls", "3 text messages."

All from an unsaved number but one she recognized, Pedro.

"No.... no no..." she mumbled.

She opened the text messages and read them silently.

"Yo you still at that Christmas thing?"

"I'm at the pool hall some squad cars just pulled up outside, I don't know what's happening"

"I'm burning everything"

Kim cursed under her breath. She grabbed her keys and quickly ran back downstairs.

"Is everything OK..." Rin asked.

"No! Let's go!" Kim roared at her.

"Go?"

"To the pool hall! You're driving! Let's go!" she said, tossing the keys to her.

She dialed a number into the phone and pulled the front door open.

"Cindy, I'll be back!" she called over her shoulder as she jetted out the door.

She speed walked towards her car followed by Rin quickly tip toeing behind her.

"Please, Terrance, pick up," she growled through her teeth.

She and Rin both got into the car and listened as the phone rang but eventually went to voicemail. Kim suddenly recalled Terrance telling her he would be spending the holidays with his parents. She cursed aloud, kicking the side of the door. Rin watched quietly, afraid of the consequences of what she had done.

Kim looked back down at the phone and began to type out a text.

"The pool hall might be hot lay low and stay away" addressed to three unsaved numbers.

As she hit send she turned and looked at Rin furiously.

"What are you doing?! Drive!" she commanded her.

Rin jumped from her booming voice and started the car.

She drove recklessly, running lights and stop signs, cutting off other drivers, and exceeding every posted speed limit until Kim commanded her to stop.

She pulled over on the side of the road. Just across the street from the mouth of the dead end road that veered off to the discreet pathway leading to the pool hall. But unlike it normally was, the road wasn't dark or quiet. It had been blocked off by a police barricade, with squad cars parked on both sides. Red and blue lights could be seen flashing through the trees and off the back of the cars.

"No...." Kim gasped.

She jumped out the car and tried to dart across the street for the opening. Rin jumped out from the other side just as quickly and caught her around her waist.

"Kim.... Kim, what are you doing?!"

"Stop, let me.... let me go!" she screamed.

"What are you gonna do?! They're not gonna let you just run through there!"

"Let go!" she grunted.

They struggled fighting against each other. Kim broke away only long enough to take a few steps before Rin was able to grab her again. She pulled her back around to the passenger side of the car.

The sound of a siren froze them both where they stood. The sound was growing, it was getting closer. They then saw an ambulance round the corner straight ahead of them. An officer stepped out of one of the squad cars and placed the barricade aside allowing it to enter.

"No!" she cried.

Kim began fighting even harder to break loose of Rin's hold on her.

"Let go!" she cried.

"Kim, stop…. stop, don't make a scene! You can't go down there!" she grunted, pulling her back.

They struggled against one another until Kim collapsed to her knees in defeat.

For the second time that night tears would stain her face, this time tears of sorrow. Her entire body went limp as she began crying harder and harder.

"C'mon Kim, get up, we gotta go before they see us," Rin said.

Kim refused to move, she remained sobbing on her knees as tears rolled down her cheeks.

"Kim, c'mon!" Rin insisted.

She stepped to the car and opened the passenger side door. She stepped back over to Kim and pulled her up from the ground forcing her back inside the car. She shut the door and ran around jumping in the driver seat. She released a breath of relief as Kim continued to ball uncontrollably. Rin could only stare ahead in silence. It broke her heart seeing her sister cry and knowing her own actions were the reason why only made it hurt all the worse. She couldn't even look at her.

Ashamed and guilt drenched she couldn't find words to speak other than the formality she had already expressed a thousand times on the ride there.

"I'm sorry Kim, I'm so sorry…" she whimpered.

Chapter 7

The Fall II

"Breaking news. An abandoned pool hall tucked off into the woods just south of Comet street was actually not so abandoned after all. The JCPD were tipped off about illegal covert operations taking place within the building yesterday. The JCPD surrounded and entered the building to find a single man of Hispanic descent destroying hundreds of documents inside. The man fired upon the officers, wounding one of them before he himself was shot and killed. None of the destroyed documents were able to be salvaged, but the JCPD plan to launch a full investigation to discover what exactly may have been taking place within the building..."

Kim grabbed the remote and clicked the television off, the news anchor's words felt like blades being jammed into her ears. A brief moment of silence lingered in the living room. Aaliyah and Charlotte had been waiting at Kim's house when she and Rin returned. Kim chose not to tell them everything she knew, claiming to have only found out after receiving texts from Pedro and then passing by seeing several police cars blocking off the road.

"Why didn't he come back?" Charlotte asked.

Her voice was weak. Her head was bowed as she wiped her face dry of falling tears.

"We were at the bar waiting. We sent him back to get some things we left. He shouldn't have been more than thirty minutes but he never came back. For some reason he stayed there."

Kim knew why. Pedro was one to grow bored quickly, he wouldn't stick around for what he already knew to be a dead stakeout. After what she had told him beforehand, she was surprised he had still went with them at all.

"Whatever the reason was, for the rest of us, it was a blessing that he didn't come back." Aaliyah said to her, "He saved all our tails. Had he not been there and burned everything, those pigs would've had everything on us. Everything The Pool's done since the beginning, they'd have had enough to throw us all under the jail."

Aaliyah's voice was flat, she was deflated as well. The spunk and excitement she normally spoke with was absent.

"I-I just can't believe it..." Charlotte whimpered.

Kim quietly backed herself into the kitchen and leaned over the countertop. Her head was pounding, her eyes were red from crying all the way home, she felt drained. She didn't know how she was even still standing.

From the corner of her eye she saw someone lean up against the countertop next to her. She turned her head and saw Helena standing there with her arms crossed. The smile that was normally plastered across her face wasn't there. Instead, she held a look of uncertainty and concern that left Kim unsettled. If even Helena wasn't smiling, she knew things must truly be bad.

"I know what you're thinking, and you're wrong." Helena said leaning close to her, "It's not your fault, there's no way you could've known."

She wanted to believe her. Part of her brain told her she was right just as she had been about everything else. It couldn't be her fault; she didn't make the call. But that part of her brain was at war with another that was telling her the blame was hers to bear. Had she killed the man the first night, told them the truth about where she knew he would be the next day, or not lost an hour running to see her parents, maybe she could've warned him in time. Maybe it could've all been prevented.

The doorbell sounded. It echoed off the walls of the mute house.

"I got it," Cindy said.

Kim pushed herself off the countertop and wiped her eyes clear of tears. Helena pushed herself up as well and disappeared down the hallway. Her somber mood was so foreign, it shook Kim more than anything else really.

Terrance came from around the corner and froze when he saw Kim. Her red eyes and tear stained face spoke the answer to his question before he even asked it.

".... he's gone, he covered us, but he's gone," Kim said.

He rushed forward and embraced her tightly. Kim wiped a few tears on his shoulder. Aaliyah and Charlotte stepped into the kitchen with pitiful looks on their also tear stained faces.

Terrance pulled back slowly holding on to her shoulders. She could tell he had been crying as well. In the nearly twenty years she had known him he had never looked more visibly shaken as he did in the moment.

"What happened?" he asked.

"I-I don't know," she mumbled, avoiding eye contact.

"Kim," he shook her gently, "you know something, otherwise you wouldn't have texted us. What happened, we can't afford to not be on the same page right now."

She thought about telling him the same lie she told Aaliyah and Charlotte but figured it would be pointless and just further complicate things. She opened her mouth to speak a few times but nothing came out. She truly didn't know where to even start. The night had already been long enough before the current incident occurred, it only served to further scramble her mental load.

"C'mon Kim, talk," he demanded, shaking her again.

"I-I..." she stuttered.

"It's my fault," Rin said, peeking out from the hallway, "it's all my fault."

All eyes in the house focused on her. Terrance looked at Aaliyah and Charlotte and raised an eyebrow. They both shrugged as neither of them had been properly introduced to her yet.

"And who the hell are you?" Terrance asked.

"I'm..." she began.

"Look," Kim moved and stood in front of Rin, "it's a long story OK. A lot has happened tonight, for us at least. This is the woman from the dockyard surveillance video."

Kim caught Aaliyah and Charlotte's reactions from the corner of her eye. Surprised, both took a step back as they looked Rin over.

".... yeah.... and she also happens to be..."

"Your sister," Terrance finished Kim's sentence.

His quick correct guess stunned Kim.

".... yeah.... how.... how'd you know..."

"When I said there were a few surprises in that envelope I gave you, she was what I was talking about. I found your name in the records of a hospital that got destroyed during the raids, the hospital you were born at. Your file led me to your mother's, and inside it said she had had two children. Both born the same day, minutes apart."

He pushed Kim aside and stepped towards Rin. He cut his eyes as he looked her up and down.

"But what do *you* have to do with this?"

Rin hesitated, she looked around the kitchen and saw she had everyone's attention. She looked at

Kim who nodded slightly. The time for withholding information had passed, the truth was suddenly invaluable beyond measure.

"I gave the police the location of you guy's pool hall."

"What?!" Terrance cocked his head.

Both Aaliyah and Charlotte's jaws dropped.

"I'm sorry I didn't know..."

"Who the hell do you think you are?!" Terrance cut her short as he began stomping towards her.

Kim quickly jumped in front of him holding him back.

"Hey, stop!"

Rin stepped out from behind the corner and held her ground.

"Just listen OK?!" she pleaded.

"Listen?! Little girl, I'll kill you!"

Kim grabbed his arm and pulled him into her. She leaned in with her shoulder pressing it directly into his chest sending him stumbling back a bit.

"No you won't. Lay a finger on her and you'll be the next one to die tonight," she said, her voice was cold and hard.

The house again fell eerily quiet. Looks of complete awe were present on everyone's face. Terrance himself shot Kim the dirtiest of looks.

"You're protecting her? After what she's done? Kim, Pedro's dead, because of her."

"She's my sister, what am I supposed to do?!" Kim screamed.

She could feel more tears coming, though she was surprised she had any left to cry.

"I know she messed up, we'll deal with that, but right now what's another body gonna do?"

"She's not wrong man," Aaliyah chimed in, "the JCPD said they're gonna launch an investigation of the pool hall. I'll believe it when I see it but realistically the lead she gave them was far from empty, so we all need to be layin low right now."

Kim and Terrance were deadlocked, staring at each other with fire in their eyes.

"We'll deal with what she did but don't you ever threaten my sister again. Don't forget which one of us has been clearing contracts the past six years."

The house again fell mute. Terrance conceded behind a nasty scowl. He may have taught her most of what she knew but if it came down to it, he couldn't take her and he knew it.

A light buzzing broke the silence. It was coming from Rin. Everyone immediately turned to her. She reached into her pocket and pulled her phone out. She looked at the caller ID and immediately her eyes rose to Kim.

"It's Greentree..."

"This late? That can't be normal for a place like that."

She answered the phone with a light hello.

"Yes.... yes.... ummm…. OK.... can you tell me what the problem is? .... OK.... OK.... we'll be there shortly.... yes.... th-thank you."

She hung up and looked around. All eyes were still on her. She looked at Kim.

"They said they need us up there as soon as possible."

"For what?" Kim asked.

"I don't know, they wouldn't tell me. They just said it was an emergency and that Mom and Dad need us."

"An emergency?" Kim asked.

"Mom and Dad?" Terrance asked.

"Our parents," Kim told him, "we're gonna have to go see what's going on."

"Whoa wait, you're leaving? With this mess going on?" Terrance questioned.

"Going on? Terrance it's over, what happened, happened. We can't fix anything. All we can do now is hope he destroyed everything that had our business attached to it before they...." Kim refused to speak the rest of her thought, "Listen we're going, OK? We'll talk when we get back."

"Everything your parents put into The Pool, how much it gave you for all these years and this happens and you just don't even care?" his voice had turned a bit soft.

Kim opened her mouth to speak before Rin stepped out in front of her.

"No, actually, her parents are downtown right now and they need her, so we're going," she said with a sharp attitude.

"Listen little girl, you better get outta my face before I..."

"Enough! Both of you!" Kim yelled, stepping in between them.

She turned to Terrance.

"Look, I hate what happened tonight OK, I really do. Pedro was more than my partner, he was like a brother to me.... he *was* a brother to me, and it's tearing me up right now that he's gone. But this is my *actual* sister," she pointed to Rin, "and those are my *actual* parents who need me right now. You know how much I've wanted this and for how long, just to meet them. Well, I met them tonight and it meant more than anything in the world to me. But they're in bad health right now and I don't know how much time I have left with them. The ones you're talking about are already gone, and you know I love them to death, but they're already gone. But the pair downtown are still here and they need me right now. I have to go."

She turned to Rin.

"I know what you were trying to do and I know you had our parents' best interest in mind. That's the only reason I'm not tearing into you right now, but you know you messed up. You put all of us in danger and cost us someone important to us. We're gonna go see about our parents right now but know, we're not done dealing with this. In fact, we haven't even started yet."

Rin nodded.

Kim looked back at Terrance, and then over to Aaliyah and Charlotte.

"Look, I'm sorry, I really am OK? Just stay here, we'll be back and we'll deal with this, I promise."

Terrance let out a huff of air and turned his back to her. Kim rolled her eyes at what she deemed to be childish behavior from him in the moment.

"We'll be here, go do what you gotta do," Aaliyah said.

"Thank you," Kim nodded.

Kim walked over to Cindy. She had been watching everything in silence the entire time. Kim placed her hand on her head.

"Hey kiddo, I'm sorry. I know this is a lot, and I know you didn't sign up for all this but..."

"Just be careful," Cindy said hugging her tight.

Kim hugged her back.

"I will. If you need anything ask one of them OK?" she said, pointing to Aaliyah and Charlotte, "I know you don't know them but they're family."

"OK," she nodded.

"I'll be back."

She stood and looked in the direction of Terrance. He was still looking out the window refusing to face her. Kim sighed shaking her head.

"Hey," Aaliyah whispered, "don't worry, we'll talk to him."

"Yeah, go," Charlotte added.

"Thanks," Kim nodded.

She turned to Rin, "C'mon."

~

Kim and Rin road in mostly silence as they traversed the freeway. They kept their focus turned away from one another avoiding eye contact. Kim stared straight as she drove while Rin looked out the window to her right. The only thing audible inside the car was the sound of the radio reporting traffic and other news.

"*This just in, the JCPD responded to an anonymous lead given regarding an abandoned pool hall down...*"

Rin turned her head slightly just as Kim reached to cut the radio off. As she did, Kim gave her a quick shift of her eyes then immediately focused back on the road. Brief as it was her glance was condemning.

"I'm sorry Kim, I really am..." she whispered.

Kim sighed, shaking her head. As much as she wanted to continue being furious with her, she knew her anger wasn't fully justified. She couldn't have known. Rin did what she believed was ultimately best for their parents, she couldn't fault her for that.

"It's fine Rin, you don't have to keep apologizing."

There was no anger or sadness in her tone, only fatigue. She couldn't remember a longer night of her life. The only one comparable would've been the night she spent trying to find Cindy and LuLu after they had been kidnapped. Yet even still, that night fell short in comparison to what the current had already put her through.

"That guy, your boss, he seemed.... upset..."

"He's not my boss," Kim corrected, "he's just the orchestrator of everything really. Don't worry about him though, he's upset but he's not gonna do anything."

"I-I just wish there was something I could..." she was cut short by another buzzing sound.

She reached into her pocket and pulled out a phone. Kim noticed it was a different phone than the one she had answered before they left the house.

She glanced at the caller ID and scoffed.

"Greentree?" Kim asked.

"No," she answered, sending the call to voicemail as she dropped the phone into her lap.

"That's not the same phone you had at the house is it?"

"No, burner phone," she said pointing to it, "got it from the guy who just called actually."

"Some guy just gave you a burner phone?"

"I mean he's not just some random guy technically. It's the guy that got me started.... killing.... the guy who hooked me up with my trainers too."

How uncomfortable she was with even speaking of the act reminded Kim of how new she was to it. She believed she couldn't have been doing it for more than just a few months.

"Yeah?"

"Yeah.... he was also the one who told me to come out here, he was the source I was telling you about earlier."

Kim cocked her head to the side as she thought for a moment.

"Back at the house, you mentioned a he, the one who suggested you get rid of everyone else out here doing what you came to do. Same guy?"

"Yep," she nodded.

Kim thought a little more before continuing.

"Was he also the one who told you to go after the man on the yacht, and the man at the bar?"

"Yeah, same guy."

"Sounds like he's feeding you contracts, I thought you were a mercenary?"

"I am, but he got me started and he was the only one paying me at the time so I figured I might as well stick with him, at least for the time being?"

"So, why not take his call?"

"Cause he's just gonna hound me for not getting anything done since I've been here. I mean, I got the guy on the boat, but whatever was supposed to be in that safe wasn't there, and the other guy is canceled so..."

"What did he say was supposed to be in the safe?"

"Just a lot more money than there actually ended up being, he said something like three to four-hundred grand cash. A cut of that was mine if..."

"And what was his reaction when you told him there was only two in there?"

Rin thought for a moment.

"Ummm.... I mean he didn't really seem all that worried about it actually. The kill was what he was more concerned with. The fact that we had an opportunity to grab a little extra cash on the side was just gonna be a bonus."

Kim was connecting details in her head. Coming to a realization Rin seemed to be completely oblivious to.

"How often do you talk to this guy?"

"Uhhh.... I don't know, he usually checks in every night or so."

"From that phone? The one he gave you?"

"Yeah?"

Kim rolled her eyes and clinched her teeth. Her calm demeanor had dissolved and left an irritated and flustered look on her face. She shook her head and cursed under her breath at Rin.

"Give it here," she huffed, extending her hand out.

"What?" Rin asked, placing the phone in her hand.

Kim rolled down the window and chucked the phone outside.

"Hey?! What are you..."

"That's not a burner phone Rin, that's a tracking device!" she cried.

"What?!"

Kim noticed Rin's eyes grow wide as she looked from Kim to something directly behind her.

The sound of metal scraping and a loud crash rang in her ears as she lost control of the car. It veered hard to the right. Kim tried bracing herself to the center console before she took a quick glance to her left and saw that they had been rammed by a black SUV. She quickly turned back as the car swerved wildly across two lanes of traffic. The sound of skidding tires, screeching brakes, and honking horns filled her ears. The car shifted to an incline position as Kim realized they had drifted off the freeway and were rolling down a hill into a densely wooded area.

Kim stepped on the break hard but she couldn't stop them in time before they crashed into a tree. They both fell into the car's airbags.

They both sat in shock for a moment, looking around ensuring they were fine. They waved the dust from the air looking around until their eyes met. With quick stares, they silently assured each other they were both OK.

Kim pulled her hair pick from her side and slashed at the airbag popping it. She then snatched the deflated bag from in front of her. She looked over and saw her door had been caved in from the hit. She tried to open it but it wouldn't budge. She growled, cursing under her breath. She twisted in her seat and pressed both her feet up against the door. She gave it four large thrusts until the door flew open allowing her to slide out the car. Rin opened her door and walked around to meet her.

Kim looked up to the freeway from where they had fallen as if waiting for something else.

"Hey, you OK?" Rin asked dusting herself off.

Kim whipped her head around and looked as if she had insulted her.

"What?" Rin shrugged.

"That was him wasn't it?" Kim asked.

"I don't know?" she shrugged again.

"Of course that was him!" Kim angrily shouted at her.

"What do you mean? Why would he..."

"You were careless! He gave you that phone so he could know where you were at all times. He's tracking you Rin, and that was his first attempt at offing you!" she howled, pointing towards the freeway.

"What? Why though? Because I didn't get what was supposed to be in the safe or kill the guy at the bar?"

"The safe was nothing but a dead lead, he didn't care about that safe or whatever was supposed to be in it. For whatever reason he wanted those two men he put you on dead, but he wanted to keep his hands clean. That's why he told you to come out here. He knew he could get you to do it for cheap and be able to keep an eye on you the whole time you were out here."

"But why'd he be coming after me now?" she asked.

"Did he already pay you?" Kim asked.

Rin nodded yes.

"Then probably because you didn't finish the job killing the guy at the bar the other night, probably thinks you're trying to take his money and run."

"OK but.... how are you so sure about all this?" she asked.

"Because we got the same two contracts at The Pool about a week or two before you showed up. It had to be him, he even told us the same thing he told you about the safe and what was supposed to be in it. It was just bait to get us to get it done quicker. He probably got tired of waiting on us, so he sent you to clean up what he hoped we would."

"Maybe it's all just a coincidence?"

"There's no such thing as coincidences," Kim snapped.

Rin was staring into space, slowly putting the pieces together herself as Kim explained everything. She looked horrified. She was shocked she had been lied to and manipulated so easily.

"Don't trust everyone who offers you help, not in this business," Kim said.

Rin turned from her, cursing herself under her breath.

"I'm sorry for causing all this mess."

Her voice was weak and timid as she apologized. The innocence in her eyes made Kim soften her frown a bit. She couldn't help but pity her. She imagined had someone else been standing there watching them they would have seen her the same way she saw Terrance when he would often scold her.

"Listen Rin…" she lightened her tone.

Before she could finish, her ear caught the sound of a running vehicle at the top of the incline from where they had fallen. Then, the sound ceased, three doors opened, and slammed back shut.

She grabbed Rin by the arm and darted for the woods behind them dragging her along.

"Whoa, where are we..."

"Just run! We don't need to be seen!" Kim shouted over her shoulder.

"What about your car?!" Rin asked.

"That's my third one this year! It's no big deal, just keep running!" Kim yelled releasing her arm.

Rin shadowed her every move as they cut through the dense green jumping over fallen trees and ducking under low branches.

Kim looked up and saw morning was starting to break. The deep blue sky told so. She still couldn't believe what the night had put her through. What she had seen, what she had discovered, it all felt like a dream that was slowly turning into a nightmare.

"How far are we going?!" Rin called up to her.

"Just keep..." Kim suddenly stopped as they came to a large grey wall standing in their path.

"I guess that's how far," Rin said stopping behind her.

Rin slumped over attempting to catch her breath as Kim stepped forward. Kim spotted a door at the bottom right of the wall and noticed a fire escape hanging on the right side.

"It's a warehouse, the back of one anyway," she said.

She cautiously walked up towards the door. She noticed an excessive amount of random junk scattered around the building. Torn up newspapers, pieces of broken plastic and glass, paper bags, random articles of clothing, and a myriad of other misplaced items scattered about.

Kim placed her ear up to the door and tried to listen.

"Nothing," she said.

She grabbed the knob on the door and slowly began to turn it surprised to find it unlocked. She slowly pushed the door open and peeked inside; it was pitch black. She couldn't see anything but a familiar sent hit her nose that caused her to pause. She took another whiff, thinking, trying to remember, before it finally hit her.

"You gotta be kidding me..." she groaned to herself.

"What?" Rin asked, "You see someone?"

Kim pulled the door open and stepped inside. She ran her hands against the wall of the warehouse until she found a light switch and flicked it on.

A loud hum began as several rows of lights hanging high above them came on illuminating the warehouse.

Inside were several unmarked wooden crates stacked high and low all around the warehouse floor.

"Is that..." Rin sniffed the air a few times.

Kim reached to her left and pulled open the crate closest to them. Inside were multiple cannabis plants.

"Tsk.... small city," Kim whispered under her breath.

"What is this place?" Rin asked.

"It's a grow house for the Colt 45s. Looks like their packing up to move all this somewhere else. Makes sense, the place was broken into a few months ago," she smirked.

They walked forward a bit to a small empty space in the middle of the warehouse where they were surrounded by towers of the crates. There looked to be easily over a hundred altogether.

"Hmph.... if all these crates are full, that's a lot of money they're sitting on," Rin said.

They both froze as they began hearing voices mumbling from what sounded to be not too far from the entrance. Kim ran back and gently closed the door they had entered from.

"Let's go," Kim whispered to her as she ran past Rin.

They sprinted back to the front end of the warehouse, bolting for the door. Kim sucked her teeth seeing the door chained and padlocked shut.

"Ugh.... really, who chain locks a building from the inside?"

They heard the back door they had entered open and smack the wall hard.

Kim pressed her back up against a wall of stacked crates. Rin followed doing the same. They both listened as their trailers entered the warehouse.

"Yo, y'all smell that?" a voice asked.

"Aye look, it's tree," another chimed in.

They heard one of the crates drop onto the ground.

"Are all these full of..."

"Aye, that ain't what we here for right now, find Rin!" a much deeper voice said.

"You sure she dipped in here?"

"The door was unlocked and the lights are on. She gotta be in here."

"Looked like there was someone else in that car with her when we hit them."

"Then they in this too."

Kim turned to Rin.

"What do you know about this guy?"

"Not a whole lot. He sold drugs and weapons around our neighborhood back home. There were always rumors that he was into a lot more than what he did back there but I never asked any questions."

155

Kim thought about the connection between him and the two men he had contracted them to kill. She knew that the other two men were connected but only by what he had told Rin.

"Those two men he asked you to kill, I think they might of been his partners in whatever he's got his hands in. He wanted them dead, probably to reap whatever benefits he could by taking out whoever he was having to share profits with," Kim whispered.

"You think so?" Rin asked.

"Wouldn't be the first time I saw a partnership end up like that," she shrugged.

Rin looked spooked. She was realizing she was simply a pawn in a game much larger than herself. She could only shake her head in shame.

"Check the left and right sides. I got y'all's back, she's in here for sure."

Kim and Rin traded gazes of urgency.

"How are we gettin outta here?" Rin asked.

Kim slowly peeked around one of the crates and caught a glimpse of their seekers.

Three men, two dark skinned and one of a lighter tone, all holding pistols.

The shortest, also the lighter skinned of the three, looked as though he were barely into his twenties. He walked timidly around as he jerked in all directions, checking his blind spots with his gun held out in front of him.

Another, a bit taller and built much larger than the other, had dreadlocks that came down his back. He walked carelessly around watching only directly in front of him with his gun down at his side.

The tallest stood in the empty space in the middle of the warehouse as he surveyed all around him. Kim assumed the deepest voice they had heard belonged to him. He was massive, in both height and mass. He was built like a tank standing well over six feet. He wore a white tank top showing off his muscular arms which were covered in tattoos and on his face, a menacing grimace

Kim pulled back around to face Rin and sighed.

"OK, they're all armed, we can't let them see us."

Rin nodded. Kim tucked her chain into her shirt and motioned for her to follow her lead.

"Keep low and keep quiet," Kim mouthed to her.

Rin nodded.

They carefully crept around the crates stacked about the floor, tip toeing along. They tried to remain as low as possible, keeping themselves out of sight.

"Anything?!" the tallest man called out.

"I don't think they came in here man!" one shouted back.

"Yeah, I don't see nothing, it's like a maze in here!" the other said.

Kim and Rin continued to sneak about the crates, eventually moving their way behind the three men.

Kim noticed Rin's focus lock as they passed by the last tank of a man standing in the middle of the warehouse. She glared hard at him as her nostrils flared, her teeth clenched, and her hands balled into fists. Kim assumed he was the one she had been talking about, the one who sent her to Joy City.

"Hey," Kim nudged her, grabbing her attention.

Rin whipped her head around to face Kim.

"The door's right there," Kim mouthed pointing just ahead of them, "you go first."

Rin nodded but before she was able to take a step she began buzzing again. Both their eyes met and their jaws dropped in unison. They quickly turned and saw the tallest of the men spin around and smirk as he caught sight of them.

"Aye yo! Got her!" he called out.

He raised his gun, pointed it at Rin, and began walking them down. Kim sucked her teeth and cut her eyes at her. Rin offered Kim a small shrug before she whipped her head back to the man closing in on them. He grabbed Rin by the arm, pulled her up, and threw her hard into a wall of crates. She grunted as she slammed against them. The man turned back and looked at Kim puzzled before grabbing her and tossing her in the same fashion.

The other two men rushed over with their guns drawn pointed at them. They stood at the tallest man's side like soldiers.

Kim turned to Rin who slowly began raising her hands. Kim did the same. The tallest man then stepped closer until he was right in Rin's face. He pressed the barrel of his gun into her stomach. Kim winced at the sight as though the gun had been pressed into her own gut.

"Talk," he said to Rin.

158

"I don't know what you wanna hear," she responded.

He pressed the gun deeper into her.

"Don't play with me Rin, why's that clown still alive? I told you exactly where to find him twice."

"He.... got away..." she mumbled.

He snickered at her response, cocked back with his free hand, and punched her in her stomach. Rin dropped her hands and hunched over holding her stomach as she groaned in pain.

"Hey!" Kim barked at him.

The man looked at Kim with the same puzzled look he had before. He stepped in front of her.

"Who are you?" he asked her.

"Leave.... her alone," Rin grunted, still holding her stomach.

Ignoring her he looked Kim over for a moment.

"She ain't just anybody, I can see that. She looks too much like you, gotta be a cousin or something," he said.

"*Sister*," Kim corrected sternly.

She stuck her neck out showing she wasn't afraid of him. He drew back a bit. She assumed it was respect rather than fear that made him do so.

"Hmph…. tough chick," he said, side eyeing her.

She fired a fierce look back at him. He stepped back over to Rin as she slowly rose back up to a standing position.

"Talk Rin."

"I don't know what you wanna hear," she insisted again.

"Why didn't you kill him?" he asked.

"I told you, he got away."

"You found a way on a private yacht crawling with security and killed a man right in his own office. I'm supposed to believe you couldn't kill a man walkin out of a bar? Do I look stupid? Last night I gave you his location again, and you bailed from the site, ended up at some diner."

Rin twisted her lips into an angry pout.

"Yeah, that's right, I got eyes all over this city. I know exactly where you've been."

"Eyes, or a tracking device in the phone you gave me?" Rin snapped back.

The man's face told that he was surprised by her knowledge that he was tracking her. He clinched the gun tightly in his hand and murmured something under his breath.

Kim looked at the two men standing behind him. Neither had their eyes on her. Both were focused on Rin. The smaller, more timid one had his gun drawn, pointed directly at Rin while the other was still holding his at his side.

"What's all this even for? You sent me out here to kill those two men for a reason, why? I'm not stupid, I know there's something bigger to all..."

"Mind your business!" he barked in her face.

He pushed the gun into her stomach again and leaned in close to her.

"You got one more time to lie to me Rin. Why didn't you kill him, why'd you bounce? I know you were right there both nights. Say somethin I don't like, and you and her are dead," he growled.

"I don't know what you wanna hear," she huffed again.

He leaned in even closer to her. She scrunched her face up and turned her head away from him.

"Alright," a malicious grin came across his face, "maybe I'll pay your parents a visit then, I'm sure they'll talk."

Rin cocked her head back and spit directly in his face. He drew back and Rin kicked him in his stomach knocking him back into the taller of the two standing behind him. They both tumbled over. Kim quickly pulled her pick from her waist and threw it into the neck of the other man still standing. He dropped his gun and fell to his knees holding his neck as blood began to spill out.

Kim and Rin made quick eye contact and began sprinting towards the door they came in from. As they made their escape they heard shots begin firing off behind them.

"Stay low!" Kim shouted as they ran.

They shielded their heads as bullets passed through the crates all around them, sending chunks of wood flying into the air.

They both dashed out the door and Kim slammed it shut behind them. She began frantically looking around where they stood. She spotted an old wooden board amongst the junk scattered about. She grabbed it and wedged it underneath the knob.

She then turned and looked at Rin furiously.

"Really?! How many phones do you have?!" she asked.

"You tossed the burner phone," she said.

A loud thud suddenly came from the other side of the door. Kim and Rin backed away quickly. They heard frustrated grunts and swears as the men attempted to bust down the door. The wooden board bent a little with each thump.

"That's not gonna hold them forever, c'mon, let's get out of here," Rin said.

"No!" Kim objected, grabbing her, "We can't let them make it out of there alive."

"Huh?"

"If he's been tracking you ever since you got to Joy City then he knows everywhere you've been, that includes my house and Greentree. If he can't find us he'll just go to one of them and we're not gonna take that risk."

"OK.... so what's the plan, cause we don't have a lot of time here?"

Kim looked around, quickly scanning the junk again until something caught her eye. She rushed over and picked up a plastic gasoline container. She shook it and rejoiced in hearing the sound of liquid swishing inside. She handed it to Rin and again started searching until she found a small lighter. She picked it up and pressed the trigger confirming it had fluid. She rejoiced again at the spark of the flame.

"What are you..."

"We're burning this warehouse to the ground with them inside it," Kim told her.

"What?"

"It's not the greatest of ideas I know, but it's the only one I got right now alright? Let's go," she said.

She walked to the right side of the warehouse and began to climb its fire escape. Rin followed closely behind her. Once they got up to the roof Kim pointed to a glass skylight.

"Watch your step, don't make too much noise," she warned.

They carefully walked over until they were standing right above the square opening. Kim knelt down next to it and watched as the two taller men continued trying to break the door down as the other stood back, still holding onto his bleeding neck. Kim lifted the latch up and carefully flipped the thick piece of glass up and over.

"Alright, let's make this quick and get gone, here's what we're gonna..."

Kim stopped and looked up as Rin's cell phone again started buzzing. Rin balanced the gas can on her hip and pulled the phone from her pocket.

"What the.... turn that thing off Rin!" Kim hissed.

"But..." she held up the phone.

"No! Turn it off!"

She turned back to the skylight and groaned, "That doors not gonna hold much longer. This might just be a waste of time."

"Hello.... yes..." Rin whispered.

Kim looked up again and saw her with her phone up to her ear.

"Are you serious right now?!" Kim asked her.

"…. what?" Rin asked into the phone.

Her stare went blank and she froze.

"Rin?! Rin?!" Kim called to her.

Still unresponsive, she continued staring into space. She then suddenly dropped the gasoline tank at her side. It fell with a loud thud that rattled the roof. Kim's jaw dropped and her eyes grew wide. She quickly turned back to the skylight and saw that the men inside had heard the sound as well.

"Aye, they on the roof!" one of them yelled.

They instantly began shooting up at them. Kim fell backwards onto her hands and scooted herself away from the skylight as bullets began ripping through the top of the roof. She looked up at Rin and saw she still hadn't moved. She was still standing motionless, staring into space.

"Rin?! Rin?! Get down!" she screamed at her.

Finally responsive. Rin slowly turned her head to face Kim but still refused to move.

"What are you doing?! Get down!" Kim demanded.

Rin's body suddenly twitched hard and her focus fell down to her leg. She had been hit. A bullet had gone directly into her left leg. Kim immediately saw the daze in her eyes, she took a long blink, and began to stumble.

"No no no!" Kim cried out as Rin began slowly tipping over.

Kim quickly sprung herself up and rushed over to catch her before she fell. Kim brushed her hair from over her face and saw that she had passed out.

"Ugh…. I miss being an only child," she huffed in between breaths.

Kim grabbed the phone she still had clutched in her hand and stuffed it into her back pocket. With bullets continuing to zip up from beneath them Kim dragged her body to the edge of the rooftop. She carefully pulled her down onto the first level of the fire escape. She struggled as she drug her body back and forth down the metal steps. Suddenly the sound of approaching sirens caught her ear. She looked out towards the streets in front of the warehouse and saw several police cars pulling into the parking lot.

"Ugh…. c'mon, give me a break," she moaned.

She assumed the police were responding to the gunshots. She was surprised they had responded at all.

She knew she couldn't afford to be caught anywhere near the warehouse with what was inside. She began to hurry, hauling Rin down the fire escape faster until she got them back on the ground. She then picked her up with both hands and carried her as she ran back into the woods they had come through earlier.

Once she felt she was out the range of anyone's sight, she stopped and propped Rin up against a tree. She fell to her knees and attempted to catch her breath. She grabbed Rin's leg and found where she had been hit. The bullet hadn't exited her leg. Kim felt a spike of pain begin emanating from her own leg just looking at the wound. She pulled out her burner phone and dialed a number that picked up on the first ring.

"Charlotte, remember the 45 grow house we broke into a few months ago? I need you to come pick me and Rin up from there right now. Bring whatever you have to treat a bullet wound, she got shot. Hurry, and don't come in from the front, the place is swarming with cops. Cut through the woods off the side of the freeway, you'll see my car."

She hung up the phone and tossed it aside onto the ground. She looked at her sister, bleeding and unconscious. She would've burst into tears if she could've, but the night had already been too long and too unkind to her. She was too exhausted mentally and physically to even bear more tears.

Chapter 8

Goodbyes

Kim was sitting up at her kitchen table with her face pressed up against her hand. Her eyes were closed, she was completely still. She was trying to forget, or remember rather, how exactly such an innocent Christmas Eve turned into such a dreadful Christmas morning.

"Hey?"

Her eyes immediately opened as she was shaken gently by her shoulder. She looked up and saw Aaliyah standing over her. She was so tired she thought she was seeing two of her initially.

"You good girl?" Aaliyah asked her.

"Yeah," she yawned, "I just.... I just really need some sleep, last night was just...."

Her voice was slow and groggy. Every word she spoke came out as if it were causing her an immense amount of pain to simply utter. She could only manage to keep her eyes halfway open. She was barely able to focus on Aaliyah standing just inches away from her.

"Charlotte stopped the bleeding and got the bullet out, Rin's gonna be fine. What happened when you two left here?"

Kim blew a gust of air from the side of her mouth and shrugged.

"If I knew exactly, I'd tell you. It was unreal, things just kept happening. We got run off the freeway, we had to run through the woods, we ended up cornered in a warehouse trying to sneak out, we got caught, next thing I know we're on the roof of the warehouse being shot at. She froze up, got hit, and went down. The police showed up and I had to carry her back through the woods to get outta sight. It just…. things just kept happening."

"Wait who ran you off the road? And who was shooting at y'all?"

"Some guy she knew or something.... I don't really know to be honest."

She turned and looked out the window. She saw that the sun had already risen. She figured it had to be at least seven. She had been up for nearly a full twenty-four hours.

"Well, glad y'all are alright, I mean, aside from the hole in her leg and all." Aaliyah said.

"You know," Kim squinted and her lip began to quiver, "I'm not sure if *alright* is really the word. I'm so tired right now I don't actually remember how I got here. The last thing I remember is sitting in the middle of the woods, looking up at the sky, and just wondering, who the hell did I piss off to deserve this nightmare of a life I'm living?"

"I'm sorry Kim, I know it's been a rough road for you."

The empathy in her tone was apparent. She could only herself imagine what Kim's life had been like, let alone what she had been through in just the past twenty-four hours.

"You hungry?" Aaliyah asked, "We made some…"

"Hey hey, aqui, she's coming to!" Charlotte called from the living room.

With a sudden burst of energy Kim jumped up from the table and rushed into the living room. Rin had been laid out on a blanket on the floor as Charlotte treated her wound. Kim, Aaliyah, Cindy, and Terrance all gathered around her.

"Watch her leg," Charlotte said to them as they crowded around her.

Kim dropped to her knees next to her and grabbed her hand. With her eyes still only halfway open Rin stared straight up at the ceiling obviously still in a daze.

"Rin? Rin?" Kim repeated softly.

She responded with a few slow blinks. Kim grabbed her face and gently turned it towards her.

"Hey hey, look at me, are you OK?" Kim asked.

After a few more blinks Rin's eyes finally focused on Kim. She squeezed her hand tightly.

"Kim?" she groaned, trying to sit up.

"Unh uh, no," Charlotte pressed her back down gently, "stay down. Keep that leg still."

Rin closed her eyes and took a deep breath. She too, was beyond exhausted.

"Hey," Kim said, gently shaking her, "what's the matter with you? What happened back there?"

"Ugh…. huh?" Rin moaned confused.

"She's still a little disoriented, you might wanna give her a minute," Charlotte said.

"No," Kim waved off her suggestion, "Rin, look at me. What happened back at the warehouse? You froze up like you saw a ghost, you could've been killed."

Rin thought hard for a moment, then her face suddenly went sour as she seemed to remember something. A look of complete disgust came over her. She began shaking her head and biting her lip as she fought to keep herself from crying. Everyone standing over her began looking back and forth amongst themselves waiting for her to speak.

"Rin? Rin, what's wrong?" Kim asked.

"They're gone Kim. The call I got…. when we were on the roof…. it was Greentree. Mom and Dad are gone," she cried.

Kim let go of her hand, and drew back from her a bit. Her mouth fell open, her stomach dropped, her heart stopped, and her body went hot. She started trembling and a single tear rolled down her cheek.

"…. what?"

~

A light round of applause echoed off the walls mixing with a last few notes being held by a sextet dressed in all white robes. They then took their seats in the small loft behind the pulpit as a grey haired black man dressed in a tuxedo stood. He walked up to the podium sitting in the pulpit and spoke into the mic attached to it.

"We'd like to thank the choir for that wonderful selection, and now before we proceed to the burial site, we will have a few final words from the children."

He spoke to a church house that was barely even half full. All eyes inside focused on the two people sitting in the front pews, Kim and Rin.

They both rose slowly. Kim walked behind Rin as she limped up to a small podium trimmed in white orchids resting in front of the congregation.

Rin leaned onto the podium taking the weight off her leg and huffed a sigh of distress. She unfolded a few pieces of paper and placed them down on the podium. She skimmed over them quickly with a twisted face. She slowly turned to her left and cringed at the two white caskets trimmed in gold, resting side by side. Kim placed her hand on her shoulder to comfort her. Rin shook her head in denial, cleared her throat, and began to speak.

"Good afternoon and thank you to everyone here. I won't be long," she assured them.

She took a final deep heave and began reading from the papers she had placed down.

"This funeral…. this *service*, at least compared to any other one I've ever been to, feels a little unique, and not just because of my relationship to the two we're here for. For the mistakes that my parents made in their lives, they were disowned by the majority of our family before I was even old enough to speak. Whatever mistakes were made that they believed were so egregious, that they could no longer pick up the phone just to say hello or even attend a homegoing service for them, still plagues their minds and hearts to this day, which is why none of them are here in attendance. My parents.... *our* parents, were not bad people. For twenty-six years, I witnessed their selflessness, kindness, generosity, and love on a daily basis. Whatever mistakes could prevent someone from being able to come say goodbye for the final time to their own cousins, aunts, uncles, brothers, sisters, I just hope that eventually they'll be able to forgive them and find it in their hearts to love them again. Because they weren't bad people, they were great people, great people who just made mistakes. But all of us are flawed beings, if we let one mistake decide how we treat someone for the rest of their life or even our own, we'd never be able to see people grow, come into their own, and become better versions of themselves. I know my parents grew, they had to. For what they went through adaptation wasn't optional, it was obligatory. They had to learn to live with their mistakes, what their mistakes cost them, learn from their mistakes to ensure they never made the same ones twice, and pass all those lessons and many more down onto me, their daughter."

She took another deep breath and another long look at the twin coffins aside her.

"They taught me so much, gave me so much, it would be impossible for me to ever truly repay them for everything they did for me."

She then turned her gaze from the caskets to Kim standing behind her.

"But as I'm forced to say goodbye to them and their physical presence in my life," she smiled at Kim, "I'm thrilled to welcome in the presence of my sister."

Kim smiled back.

"Her strength, encouragement, and exemplary attitude has kept me sane this past week, allowed me to continue living through this hard time, and I'm beyond grateful to now have her in my life. I love you Kim."

"Love you too," she mouthed back with a smile.

"And to all of you," Rin said, turning back to the congregation, "I love and appreciate you all as well. Be you friends or family of the like, thank you for being here and thank you for your condolences, prayers, and well wishes during this difficult time for us."

She paused and turned taking one last look at the caskets.

"Mom, Dad, I love you, thank you for everything."

A small short applause came about as she grabbed the papers resting on the podium and took a step back relinquishing the floor to Kim. She stepped forward to the podium delivering the same heavy exhale as Rin had. She scanned all around the church house, studying the faces of all inside. She made eye contact with every person and smiled ever so slightly before she began to speak.

"Good afternoon and thank you to all of you here. I uhhh.... I don't have anything written because, well, anyone who knows me knows I'm not much of a public speaker but..."

She paused, taking her own moment to view the caskets aside her. She took a few breaths to collect herself, cleared her throat, and continued on.

"The unfortunate truth is I didn't know my parents, not all that well anyways. Most of you know this. But thanks to this one right here," she smiled looking back at Rin, "I've gotten to know them a lot over this past week, through the sharing of stories and memories. I can confidently say I come from good stock. As my sister mentioned, these people, as great as they were, weren't perfect. Mistakes were made that cost them a lot, but the cost is what you atone for, and as scary as that can seem, it's necessary for us to pay those costs to grow as people, and so we shouldn't run from them. Not that we could anyway. I've made my fair share of mistakes in this life, committed my sins, and I couldn't be further from a saint, but the pain I've endured in just this past week alone.... has felt like the facing of twenty-six years' worth of demons all at once. But I'm still here."

She looked back in the direction of the caskets.

"Mom, Dad, I'm so sorry *this*, is our second conversation of my adult life, it shouldn't have been this way. You weren't able to watch me grow up, I imagine you had to be worried sick every moment of your lives, wondering where I was, how I was doing, if I was even still alive. I can relate. But, I want you to know over these past twenty-six years, I wasn't alone, I was taken care of. I'll give you the short version. Nearly two decades ago I somehow found myself welcomed into a family made up of people just like me, a foster home."

She looked out into the congregation and saw Ms. C, and Blake sitting together.

"And then by some miracle this beautiful couple decided I was actually cute enough to take home."

She got a light laugh out of the audience. Her foster parents' faces quickly flashed in her head bringing about an even bigger smile than the one she was already wearing.

"Everything was so perfect, they were so perfect. For about ten years I lived a life most people would've called a dream, but atonement for one's mistakes is necessary and no matter how hard you try, you'll never outrun it. Eventually their demons came for them, and just like that, they were gone. Sending me back to my first family, with a few new faces I'd soon come to know very well."

She looked at LuLu who smiled back at her.

"But I lived through that and added one to that family who welcomed me in so long ago." she looked at Cindy and smiled, "She's a real good kid, I really wish you could've met her."

Cindy smiled back.

"Through just living life, just trying to make it day to day, I met some strangers who've over time become extended family of mine. People who served as my voice of reason or just kept me grounded when I was ready to jump off the edge."

She looked at William and Max sitting on one side of the church and then to Aaliyah and Charlotte sitting on the other. She then shifted her focus to Terrance sitting alone in the back of the church.

"Those I couldn't express to enough just how grateful I am to have them in my life. Even the few I lost along the way."

She closed her eyes and saw Joey and Pedro's faces. The memories of them stung, nearly bringing a tear to her eye.

"I say all this to say," she turned to her parents as she spoke to them, "I wasn't alone these past twenty-six years. Your prayers, your hopes, your wishes, they were all answered. I was sent so many angels over my lifetime. I had family, I had people who cared and looked out for me every step of the way."

She looked up and smiled big as she caught sight of Helena sitting in the back most pew. On her face, the same beautiful smile she had eight months ago in the grocery store.

"Some I honestly couldn't even begin to explain to you."

Taking a deep breath, she turned back to her parents one last time.

"I know we weren't able to have the relationship we should've had, but I love you both regardless, and I thank you for everything I know you would've done for me had things been different. And don't worry, I promise I'll take care of Rin, we'll be OK."

She faced back forward and smiled at her friends and family.

"Thank you to all of you here for your love and support, we truly truly appreciate it."

Another light round of applause came as she stepped from behind the podium. She walked slowly behind a limping Rin as they made their way back to their seats. As they passed by the caskets Kim reached her hand out and gently drug her fingers across the tops of both.

"Bye Mom.... bye Dad," she whispered.

Chapter 9

Family III

Kim sat atop The Hill with her back hunched over, hugging her knees. She was overlooking Joy City. Such a dirty city it was on the inside, yet from the top of The Hill, under a bright orange setting sun, even she sometimes could mistake it as a beautiful place.

In her hand she held a single daisy she had picked from a bed of them on the climb up. She had picked it because it was different. It didn't fit in with the rest around it. One of its petals looked to have been torn off and its stem was crooked causing it to slump over a bit. It looked damaged, hurt even, but despite its impairments it still managed to stand on its own amongst the others. She found the thought a bit silly as it crossed her mind, but she felt somewhat akin to the flower, she felt she could relate to it.

A large gust of wind pried the flower from between her fingers. It flew twirling about in the air until it disappeared over the cliff. She imagined if it could've spoken, it would have told her thank you for rescuing it, for setting it free.

Next to her rested a balled up newspaper.

Its headline read, "THREE ARMED MEN ARRESTED INSIDE WAREHOUSE FULL OF CANNABIS".

The paper was over a week old. While the past few months hadn't been her favorite ones, and the past week had proven to be one of the most challenging of her entire life, Kim found herself in a place she couldn't remember having been in for a long time, a good place. Despite all, she was well rested, at peace, and content.

She had been sitting, looking out to the city from the hilltop for nearly an hour. She had done so every day since her parents' passing. She sat quiet, completely still as she looked out over the cliff, only blinking or releasing an occasional sigh. It was so quiet, so peaceful. Her only company the entire week had been the rustling leaves above her head and the wind. She thought about trying her hand at meditation again, but the thought of closing her eyes and missing a second of the gorgeous sunset in front of her made her decide against it. It was too beautiful to miss, and she had promised herself a while ago she would stop obsessing, stop living blind, and start to appreciate the small things in life.

Suddenly a sharp pain in her head told her to look left. Helena stood smiling down at her. She dropped down, taking a seat with her legs crisscrossed on the grass next to Kim. They both watched the sunset in silence for a moment. The warm amber light shone on their faces as the wind gently tossed their hair and clothes about.

"Beautiful service today," Helena whispered.

"It was," Kim said, her voice stark and low, "thanks for coming."

Helena giggled a bit shaking her head.

"Well, you were there, so I didn't necessarily have a choice."

"Right." Kim remembered, "Where you been, haven't seen you much this past week."

"You had a lot goin on, funeral planning, sisterly bonding and what not, I didn't wanna bother."

"Hmph.... *you* didn't wanna bother?" Kim asked with a slight laugh, "Things really are changing."

Helena playfully rolled her eyes.

"Y'all speak with Pedro's family yet?"

Kim sighed heavily at her question.

"We all went over there and explained everything to them. It was hard, they were shocked to say the least, but they also suspected he was into some dirt. Terrance apologized to them a million times, we all did. Regardless of how far the investigation of the pool hall actually goes there's a good chance they'll be questioned a lot more in the coming weeks than they've been in just this past one. Terrance assured them if they kept quiet about everything he'd make sure they never had to worry about anything ever again. He was family to us, so that makes them our family too. He said he'd personally make sure they never went without anything ever again."

"Hmph...." Helena smiled, "a bit scary looking

sometimes but he's got a good heart."

"He's always been like that, likes to play tough but outside of The Pool, he just wants the people he holds close to be OK and he'll go above and beyond to ensure that they are."

"Speaking of The Pool..." Helena asked.

Kim rolled her neck and cleared her throat.

"It's dead." she said, "Terrance decided it wasn't worth trying to salvage. Losing my foster parents was tough for him. They all built The Pool from the ground up together. I guess I kinda helped fill that void once he was gone but Pedro.... Pedro was like a son to him. He treated us all like his own. It's funny how willing he was to take on the risks that came with sending us out on contracts every other night, but I don't know that he'd ever actually prepared himself to have to deal with the possible consequences of those risks. You'd think losing my foster parents would've prepared him for that but no. That's why he's suffering now over Pedro and having a tough time with a lot of resurfacing memories and emotions."

"Well.... all good things must come to an end I guess." Helena stood up, brushing grass off her shorts, "Like me."

"Like you?" Kim raised an eyebrow looking up at her.

"Yep, sorry babe, we had a good run but I'm breaking up with you," she smiled.

"Wait, what?" Kim asked puzzled.

She suddenly spotted a figure approaching from behind her out the corner of her eye. She turned around completely to see Rin limping up The Hill towards her. She looked back and Helena was gone. She sucked her teeth.

"Next time, how bout somewhere with a little less incline sis?!" Rin called to her out of breath.

Kim rose and rushed over to help her.

"What are you doing, you're not supposed to be walking on that leg, especially not up a hill," Kim told her.

"I'm fine, it's just a little sore," she said waving off her help.

The two of them began walking back over to the cliff's edge.

"How'd you know I was up here?" Kim asked.

"Saw you head up here a couple times this week, this is the first day my leg actually let me follow you up here though."

They came to the edge of the cliff and stopped.

Rin whistled, "I see why you like it up here, nice view. Almost makes you forget how nasty it is down there."

"Yeah.... almost," Kim said, sitting back down.

She curled herself up in a ball hugging her knees again with her chin tucked behind them. Rin carefully rested herself down next to her. She gently nudged her shoulder grabbing her attention.

"Hey.... you OK?" she asked.

Kim nodded yes.

Rin scooted closer to her, "Promise?"

She nodded again.

"How bout you?"

She took a moment to collect her thoughts

before answering.

"Honestly, I don't even know. It's tough, for them to both go at the same time like that, what'd the mortuary guy call it?"

"Broken Heart Syndrome."

"Is that even real? Sounds like somethin made up."

"From what I looked up there's some science behind it that supports it but I don't really know to be honest," Kim said.

"Tsk.... some trip," Rin sighed.

"Well, what are your plans now?" Kim asked.

"Well for one, I think I'm done with this mercenary thing. I don't think it's for me."

"Good, trust me, I spent six years doing it, it's not a path you wanna go down, as you can see it can get pretty messy."

"Yeah.... when I killed that guy on the boat, I.... I almost threw up, I-I just don't think I can do something like that again."

"Well good, you shouldn't. But I mean aside from that, where are you going from here, back east?"

Rin leaned back and thought for a moment.

"Hmmm.... I don't really know, most of my adult life has kind of revolved around taking care of Mom and Dad, even before I moved back in with them. I had to turn down a lot of job offers and opportunities because I wasn't able to leave them by themselves. But now, I guess I'll go back home and just play it by ear."

"You know.... you don't have to go back," Kim

told her.

Rin's eyes widened and a small smile came to her face.

"I mean, Cin already loves having you here, I love having you here, Mom and Dad are here now.... what reason do you really have to go back?"

Rin took another moment to think.

"I mean yeah, but.... I don't have the money to make a move across the country..."

"Don't worry about that, money's not an issue, not for me anyway. Whatever you need, whatever you have back there, I'll cover whatever it cost to get it sent out here. It's just me and Cin so that extra room in the house will always be open for you, you can stay as long as you need to."

Rin's eyes lit up and her smile grew.

"Thanks."

"Of course, you're my sister.... unfortunately," she teased

"Hey, c'mon, I'm not that bad," she smiled.

"What? You're a disaster, do you realize how much you put me through in just a week?" Kim laughed, "You threw a knife at my hand, one at my head, elbowed me in the face..."

They both shared a laugh.

"Just a little sisterly scrap.... which I won by the way."

"What? No way!" Kim argued lifting her head.

"Ummm.... yes I did?" Rin nodded, "If I remember correctly you had your hands up."

"You pointed a gun at me, you cheated!"

"You had it pointed at me first!"

"But whose gun was it?" Kim raised a brow at her.

Rin rolled her eyes.

"Whatever, we'll call it a draw for now. We'll set round two for Valentine's Day." she smiled.

Kim shook her head laughing.

They watched the sunset together in silence for a bit. Listening to the wind whipping around them, the leaves rustling above them, and cars speeding on the roads down below them.

"Were Mom and Dad strict?" Kim asked.

Rin was surprised by her abrupt inquiry.

"Uhhh.... no, not really. They were really protective but overall pretty chill, let me do just about anything that wouldn't kill me. Why?"

"Just wondering," she said, tucking her chin back behind her knees.

"Kim.... you sure you're OK?" she asked again.

Kim exhaled and closed her eyes. She turned and looked at Rin.

"If I said no, would it change anything?" she murmured.

"I'm sorry Kim, I really wish you would've had more time with them."

"It's fine," she sighed, "I'm just glad I was able to meet them."

Rin leaned into Kim throwing one of her arms around her shoulder and the other under her arm locking them in front of her chest. She rested her head on Kim's shoulder.

"You know, Mom use to always swear, before she left this earth, she was gonna see you again. Dad would always tease her saying she was crazy and ask her how it was ever gonna happen, she would always say she just knew she would. How? I don't know, but she just knew it."

Kim smiled listening to her. Rin's many stories and tellings of their parents had become like medicine for her over the past week. Each one aiding in her healing more and more.

"God they were wonderful people Kim, they really really were. They showed me so much love and support and I know they would've done the same for you had they been able to. I miss them so much."

"Yeah.... me too," Kim said.

Kim stared back off into the distance. Rin looked at her and hugged her tighter.

"Hey, tell me about your foster parents," she said.

"What?" Kim smiled.

"Yeah, tell me about them. I mean I hardly know anything about your life prior to a week ago. I've been telling you all about my childhood and how I grew up, what was it like for you being brought up out here?"

Kim blew air out her mouth shaking her head as she grinned.

"Ugh.... twenty-six years in Joy City, where do I even begin?" she laughed.

~

Kim opened her bedroom door and yawned. She glanced at the clock on the wall and read the time, "1:24."

With things calming down she had finally managed to get herself on a somewhat healthy sleep schedule. However, she still found herself waking up in the middle of the night unable to fall back asleep. As usual she had only one remedy for the matter, a glass of tea.

She quietly tip toed past Cindy's room and headed downstairs. She walked into the kitchen and flicked on the light. She groaned at the sight of her sink full of dishes. She decided to save them for the morning, hopefully getting some help from either Cindy or Rin.

She walked over to the cabinet where she kept her tea but paused as something caught her eye. She walked over to the refrigerator and froze in place in front of it. Rin had placed her photo of their parents over top of Kim's destroyed copy. She wondered how long it had been there, how many times she had walked by or stood right in front of it in the past week. She found herself unable to look away from it, it was mesmerizing to her.

She still couldn't believe after all the days, months even, she had spent looking for them, they came to her with a sister she didn't even know existed. They looked so happy in the photo, all of them, so complete. Rin and her both sharing subtle smiles as their parents cheesed for the camera. She wondered how long before she was separated from them had the photo been taken. She and Rin looked as though they couldn't have been more than just a few months old. She began to imagine the grief, the absolute mental and emotional torment her parents had to suffer for twenty-six years. She could only hope the fifteen or so minutes that they spent together, all of which she wept uncontrollably for, was enough for them, was worth the wait for them.

She was infinitely grateful to have been able to meet them, if for nothing else than the opportunity to have even a single memory of them, yet she couldn't help but feel a bit empty as well. She had met them and it meant everything to her, but had just as quickly lost them in the same night. She again couldn't help but wonder what wrong she had done onto someone or something. She figured she had to be being punished for something, it was the only explanation that made sense to her.

She leaned forward resting her head against the refrigerator door. She closed her eyes and sighed. She was growing sick of her constant conflicted emotional state. As infrequently as her moments of happiness came, sorrow never seemed to be too far behind them.

"I know it's cold but that's not gonna help the headaches."

Kim clinched her teeth and shut her eyes tighter in response to the voice. There was only one voice that made her wince like that. She spun around in place.

"Up early again huh?" Helena smiled from the table behind a glass of tea.

Kim slowly made her way over to the table and sat down across from her.

"Sorry, I'd have made you a glass too but there

was only enough for one," Helena said.

Kim stared at her hard. Looking her up and down with curious eyes. Helena eventually noticing, drew back a bit.

"Whoa, take a picture K, it'll last longer," she laughed.

"On The Hill, after the funeral, you said..."

"Yeah yeah, I know," she said, setting her glass down, "you wanna know where your best friend is going..."

Kim answered with a silent stare that begged for more.

Helena pulled her beanie down a bit and frowned. This immediately alarmed Kim. She hadn't seen many emotions from Helena that didn't line up with the smile she normally had on. The one time she had the week prior things were at their worst. Helena looked off to her side, scratching her chin as she thought. Kim wasn't sure what to expect out of her mouth next. Since she showed up, rarely did she ever seem to be at a loss for words.

"Ummm.... Kim.... are you happy?" she asked.

Kim could hear her trying to speak over the lump in her throat. It almost sounded as if she were about to cry.

"Happy?" Kim repeated, "Ummm.... I mean, sure?"

Helena smiled and shook her head at her.

"I'mma need a more convincing answer than that babe."

"Why?" Kim asked.

"Just.... are you happy Kim?" she asked again.

Kim thought for a moment, curious of the angle she seemed to be taking. She remembered her telling her she never asked a question of her she didn't already know the answer to.

"I-I guess so?" Kim stuttered.

"Why? What's making you happy right now?" Helena asked.

"Are you gonna answer my question?" Kim asked.

"Relax, I'm getting to it but I need you to answer mine first. Right now, why are you happy?" she asked.

She had to think for a moment. She fell back into her chair and stared at the ceiling letting her mind run wild.

"Take your time, we got all night," Helena smiled taking another sip of tea.

"I mean, I guess cause my life is finally slowing down. I feel like after completely losing it ten years ago, I'm finally starting to regain control of it again."

"How so?"

"I mean, as bad as things turned out, I guess I got everything I asked for. The Pool is behind me, Cindy is safe, and I got to meet my parents. That still doesn't even feel real to say. I really met them, touched them, spoke to them."

Helena's smile turned into a haughty grin as she listened to her speak.

"Yeah, what else?" she asked.

"Rin, my sister.... who'd have guessed?"

"Sometimes life gives you exactly what you

didn't know you needed or wanted," Helena said.

"Yeah.... yeah, I guess so. I guess I am happy. I feel at peace for once, I feel calm. I haven't felt that in years. I gotta be happy, this has gotta be happiness," she said with a smile.

Her voice reigned with confidence, there was no uncertainty in her tone. She was happy, and although she had lost a lot, she was content with what she had.

Helena continued smiling back at her.

"I'm happy for you K, I really am. All I ever wanted was to see you happy, see you smile..."

She closed her eyes and her lip began to quiver. Her entire body twitched and she exhaled deeply.

"...and now that I have, now that you are.... I have to go," her voice cracked.

Kim's smile immediately faded.

"What? What do you mean go?" Kim asked.

Helena took another deep breath to keep herself composed. She appeared to be fighting back tears. The sight had Kim at a loss.

"Kim, remember, I'm not real, I'm just a vessel for your poisoned mind to speak through. I took form because you cast away your emotions, because you rejected your happiness, your good will, all of those emotions became me. I am you, the part of you that you shed to be the cold hearted killer you chose to be six years ago. But you just told me you're happy, and so now, I have no purpose anymore."

"No purpose? What do you mean?"

"Eventually I'll fade back into your

subconscious, for good."

A knot formed in Kim's stomach. As annoying as she initially had been, Kim had grown to like her, love her even. She couldn't imagine not having her constantly babbling in her ear.

"But hey, no more headaches right?" she smiled, attempting to relighten the mood.

Kim was unphased by her attempt at humor.

"When?" she asked.

"I don't know. Truth be told Kim, I don't know much about myself or what I am. When I showed up in the grocery store that night, I don't remember where I was or what I was before that moment I ended up in front of your cart. But somehow, I knew who you were, I knew I was there to help you, and I knew everything about you and your life."

The new truth she was speaking left Kim in wonder.

"I probably gave off the impression that I knew everything about our connection but truthfully, I didn't then and I still don't. My guess would be I knew you because well, I am you, a part of you at least. Your emotions are what gave me life. I knew I was here to help you because from the moment I began to exist we were naturally drawn together, that's why I was always able to show up wherever you were. Your brain was seeking to regain the half of it you cast out, probably because it's just designed that way. The whole is greater than the sum of its parts, it wanted to be whole again. I believe that's why I knew everything about you, what I was supposed to be helping you with was reconnecting those halves, the half you retained and the half that became me."

"I-I can't.... I..." Kim stuttered.

"Yeah.... I think that's it Kim. Your brain created me to help fix itself. Your work in The Pool was killing it. I was supposed to help you find that happiness again, breathe life back into that brain that was just being fed blood and death every single day. I guess that's why I'm naturally so goofy and light hearted, to balance things out between us, to 'offset' you and what you still were. But now that your happiness is back, your brain's no longer suffocating, you don't need me anymore. I'm gonna disappear. I don't know when, I don't know how, but I only existed to bring you happiness, to reconnect the halves. That's done now, why would I continue to exist?"

Her voice was flat as she spoke her words. No excitement or joy in her tone. Kim had never seen her so serious, so emotionally absent.

"I…. I really can't catch a break," Kim whimpered.

"Hey, don't go actin like you'll miss me now," Helena grinned.

Kim bowed her head in sorrow. Helena saw the expression and her grin faded.

"Hey, don't do that, no moping. If it helps at all, it's not like I'm dying, I'm just going back inside you.... or…. nevermind, that sounded wrong. I'm sorry, I mean you're a nice girl and all don't get me wrong but..."

Kim laughed aloud at her stumbling over her

words.

"Whoa, did I just make you laugh?"

"Shut up," Kim murmured back.

"Mission accomplished Helena, and it only took eight months," she smiled.

"I am gonna miss you, I really am," Kim said.

Helena's eyes grew wide and her mouth fell open.

"Awww…. babe?" she whined behind exaggerated puppy dog eyes and a pout.

"You know what, I changed my mind, the sooner you leave the better," Kim rolled her eyes.

"I'll miss you too," she laughed, "but I'm glad you're happy, that's so much more important to me than me being out here buggin you every day."

Helena picked up her glass and took a sip of her tea.

"So wait, tell me something…" Kim began.

"Mmhmm…" Helena hummed behind her glass.

"You said you knew everything about me when you showed up, I assume you meant my past, but did you know anything regarding my future? Like, I remember you warned me about Joey, you warned me not to get too obsessed searching for my parents, but you said you didn't know Cindy and LuLu were gonna get kidnapped. Did you know about Rin and all this craziness she was gonna bring with her? Like, I still don't fully understand what it is you know and what you don't."

Helena's stare told she was intrigued by Kim's question. She placed her glass back down on the table and covered her mouth with both hands as she looked off into space. She eventually turned to Kim and smiled.

"OK, like I've said before, I'm not a psychic and I'm not a fortune teller, but I am intuitive, that's one of the things I got from you. I can't tell you I knew then or know of anything now that hasn't happened yet, but I can tell you I feel like your happiest days are yet to come and are closer than you think. Look forward to them, enjoy them."

While it wasn't quite the answer she was hoping for her words still brought a slight smile to her face.

"Thanks," Kim nodded.

Helena nodded back

"And oh.... almost forgot."

She reached down into the pocket of her shorts and pulled out Kim's hair pick. She slid it across the table to her. Kim caught it just as it reached the table's edge.

"You left that in that guy's neck last week, might wanna clean it off first it's still a little bloody."

"I don't remember grabbing..."

"You did, don't worry about it, a lot of things were happening that night, and pretty fast at that."

She gripped the pick tightly in her hands and released the blade.

"So, speaking of your future, you plan on ever using that again?" Helena asked.

Kim retracted the blade back in and placed the pick down on the table.

"I don't know.... I don't want to."

"Then don't Kim, you have a choice. The Pool isn't a thing anymore, you have literally no obligation to."

"Yeah.... I know but..."

"Still thinkin about your foster parents huh?"

Kim buried her face in her hands.

"Kim, those people loved you, you know that. I can't imagine two people loving someone the way they loved you wanting that life for them. We don't know what led them to it but we know as great of people as they were, The Pool was their biggest sin and it's a shame it trickled down to you, but you got out with your life. They weren't so lucky. Why keep playing with it? Hasn't it cost you enough already?"

"Terrance said they meant to introduce me to it eventually, but..."

"You don't believe that. I know you don't believe that because *I* don't believe that, you're too smart to believe that. Terrance said what he said but now *I'm* telling you, your foster parents *did not* want nor did they ever intend for you to join The Pool. Now, if you'd like to waste your breath telling me I'm wrong, go right ahead, but before you do, tell me this, what have I ever been wrong about? I'll wait," Helena picked her glass back up and sipped her tea with an imperious smirk on her face.

"Yeah but..." Kim looked down at her hair pick.

"If you ask me it's cute and practical enough for it to have just been a gift. It's not like it's a sword, it's not like the only thing it can be used for is murder. Besides, he probably didn't think you'd ever figure out there was a blade inside of it anyway. In fact you didn't, Terrance had to show you that."

Kim surrendered any further argument she thought she had; she knew she had no chance of winning against her.

"Yeah, I guess you're right, I should be happy it's all behind me now, happy both me and Rin made it out on the other side of all that alive."

"Yeah, speaking of Rin, it's good she's over it too cause that life really ain't for her, that girl's no killer," Helena said.

"She told me she killed like two back east before she came out this way, and there was that guy on the yacht last week," Kim said.

"Yeah, but a dead clock is right twice a day. Plus, who else has she killed?"

"Well I kinda got in the way of what would've been her second out here," Kim reminded her.

"True but you still ended up on your back that night. Had she really wanted that kill she'd of gotten it even if it meant catching another body, yours, on top of it, but instead she ran. In the six years you were doing it how many times did you just run from an easily confirmable kill?"

The answer was zero.

"Both times you showed up and blocked her from killing that man she fell back, she didn't engage. Not to mention when she had you on your knees at gunpoint rather than just execute you, she decided she wanted to know who you were and needed to unmask you. I don't know, I just don't see a real reason to want to know who you're about to kill if you're gonna kill them regardless. I read that as her stalling, just hoping to find a reason to not have to do it, and as fate would have it, the reason found her."

Kim thought for a moment realizing she had a point. Rin had shied away from conflict as long as she could. She only fought once Kim had her cornered.

"I'm just saying," Helena shrugged, "you saw how uncomfortable she was just talking about her first kill, and she said herself sticking a knife in that guy's back on the yacht made her sick to her stomach. She couldn't even handle seeing a bullet in her leg, how's she supposed to be a killer?"

"I think she gets it, she saw how volatile it can be. She was desperate, she just wanted to be able to take care of our parents but now I think she's just looking for the next phase of her life. I'm hoping we can help each other out with that, she agreed to stay for a while to figure things out."

"You'll find it, both of you, you both just got relieved of a lot of stress and pressure. Just take it one day at a time," Helena said.

"Yeah…. It's weird though, this moment, this feeling," Kim said.

"Explain."

"Like, it's kinda terrifying, my whole life just changed in the blink of an eye."

"Change is what you wanted though right?"

"Yeah but…."

"Nope, no buts." Helena shook her head, "It's called The Law of Attraction. You bring about what you think about, good or bad. You expended so much energy searching for change, obsessing over it, the universe finally said OK, and gave you what you asked for, maybe not necessarily what you wanted, but what you asked for."

"I mean yeah, but this kinda change though? People are gone, I had to have this insane talk with Cindy about The Pool and trust the other day and..."

"Which by the way I applaud you for," Helena interrupted, setting her glass back down, "we never actually talked about that. That took a lot of prowess to have that conversation with her and it absolutely needed to happen, for both of you."

"I don't know how I feel about it honestly," Kim huffed palming her forehead.

"The Law of Attraction doesn't aim to please the heart, it bends to the will of the mind. Your mind begged for change, the universe delivered it."

Kim sighed and shook her head; she was obviously far from content.

"What's all that huffin and puffin about?" Helena asked.

"Nothin, just..." her sentence trailed off into silence.

She looked and saw Helena smugly grinning, waiting patiently for her to finish.

"We've been over this K, you can't lie to me. I already know what's on your mind but I can't answer what you don't ask."

"Right.... ummm.... do you believe in balance?"

"Balance?" Helena repeated.

"A long time ago I read somewhere that everything in the universe has an echo, every thought, action, occurrence, it's all mirrored by something that serves to retain balance in the universe."

"OK.... and..." Helena asked.

"I feel like the universe is having a little too much fun balancing my life, it almost feels like I'm being picked on. It's like I can't even enjoy lunch without coming outside to a boot on my car. Every time something good happens it's immediately followed by two more bad things."

Helena laughed at her claim.

"Universal balance is a real thing Kim, but I think you're thinking far too deep into it. I don't think you're being picked on, I think somehow you've just managed to consistently be the most unlucky person in the universe for like two decades. It's honestly pretty impressive if you think about it."

Kim rejected her humor again.

"Never mind," she breathed.

"Hey, I'm joking," she smiled, "Kim you're just living life. I promise you you're not the only person on this earth who feels that way. You're not even the only person in this house that feels that way. You don't think Rin feels picked on too? Kim, the same thing that just happened to you, happened to her too. She met her sister, and then the next day her parents died. Just because she had them in her life doesn't mean her life was perfect. The girl was driven to murder for survival, she didn't believe she had a choice. You started killing people because you thought that's what your foster parents wanted. There's a huge difference there. Not to mention, *she* got shot that night, you meanwhile walked away with a tiny little cut on your hand."

Kim hadn't given much thought to what she was saying but she knew she was right. While Rin had the one thing Kim longed for the most in her life, she lacked so much of what Kim had most of hers.

"Yeah, I guess you're right," she said.

"Of course I'm right, I'm brilliant," she said, taking another sip from her glass.

Kim was intrigued at how she took claim of her brilliance with such confidence. The way she delivered every word she spoke was entertaining to her. Her charisma and charm were unlike that of anyone else she had ever met, it was contagious. She wondered if people had viewed her that same way once upon a time.

"Above all else Kim, you just told me you're happy right now, so be happy. Don't keep looking back on the stuff that was keeping you from being happy, that's so counter intuitive."

"I'm not trying to, but it's hard you know. I can't help but get caught up in wondering how things could've been, how they would've been, wishing things had been different."

Helena looked at her with a scolding glare. She was obviously displeased with her response.

"Kim, finish this sentence for me. Life is..."

".... short?" Kim shrugged.

Helena shook her head no.

"Wrong. Life, life is *long* Kim. So long in fact

it's what the law calls a sentencing that never ends, *life* in prison. See, life can be cut short, but if it's able to play out in its entirety, life, life is long. Too long to live with regret, too long to be wondering what if, too long to keep looking back on the things you can't change. If life were short, we could wonder these things for some time and figure out what we can, take zero risks and not have to worry about regret or thoughts of what could've or would've been, because at the end of the day none of it would really matter, cause it'd all be over soon regardless. But that's not how it works, that's not how life works. Life is long, really long. Christmas Eve to Christmas morning felt like an eternity just watching from your head, I can't imagine what it physically felt like to you and Rin. If one night can last that long how can life be short?"

Kim allowed everything she said to spin inside her mind for a moment. She couldn't argue, dispute, or challenge anything. She just nodded.

"You're right.... you are brilliant," Kim whispered.

Helena shrugged behind a smile.

"It'll take time, it's hard to not remember, desire, or wish for things, near impossible actually. But in time you'll come to fall in love with what you have and you'll be able to find comfort and peace in what you don't."

Helena took one last huge gulp from her glass and slid it across the table to Kim. She looked down and saw it was empty.

Kim picked up the glass, stood, and walked it over to the sink. She placed it down on top of a mountain of other dishes that needed washing.

She turned around and jumped back a bit as Helena stood right in her face. She looked into her eyes and saw a seriousness she wasn't use to from her.

"If I've said nothing worth anything in the past eight months to you, Kim.... just let yourself be happy. You've been through too much, lost too much, to not allow yourself at least that. For the first time in a long time you're free, free from everything that's ever bound you, take advantage of that. Take advantage of this time..."

She lifted her finger and pressed it into Kim's chest.

".... be happy Kim," she gently poked her as she spoke each word.

They traded warm smiles.

"Just don't forget where you came from," she added.

Kim wiped her hand from her chest and threw her arms around her. Helena's body immediately went stiff, shocked by her embrace, but eventually returned her hug.

"Yep, that's long overdue," she laughed.

"Should I worry you won't come back?" Kim asked.

"I hope I don't come back. If I'm out here that means somethings wrong up here." she said patting Kim's head. "I'd much rather never exist again if it means you're living happy and with a sound mind."

"Will I forget you when you disappear?"

"Should I worry you'll forget?" Helena asked.

They shared a laugh.

"I don't know to be honest with you," Helena said, "but my gut tells me no. I mean how could you, I'm delightful."

Kim laughed as she squeezed her tighter.

"Thank you Helena, for everything."

Kim smiled as she thumbed away a tear rolling down her cheek.

~

"Kim.... Kim?! Kim?!"

Kim jerked her head up from the kitchen table batting her eyes wildly. Rin was standing over her with a concerned look on her face.

"You good?" she asked slightly smiling.

"Ummm.... yeah." Kim said, rubbing her eyes, "What time is it?"

"A quarter to ten, you been down here all night?" she asked.

Kim looked out the window and saw a blue sky and clouds outside. She couldn't even recall resting her head down on the table last night. All she could remember was speaking with Helena.

"Yeah.... I guess so..." she murmured.

"Everything OK?"

"Yeah, I just had a lot on my mind I guess."

She stood to her feet and the room started to spin a bit. She stumbled in place for a moment. Rin grabbed her arms holding her up.

"Kim?!" she cried.

"I'm alright, I just.... got up too fast."

"Alright..." Rin said unsure.

The sound of footsteps on the stairs turned both of their attention to Cindy trotting down with her eyes glued to her cell phone screen.

"Mom, Aunt Lu said she was texting and calling you all last night and you didn't answer."

"We live ten steps apart from each other why didn't she just walk over here?" Kim asked.

Cindy shrugged.

"Tell her I'll give her a call a little later."

"Alright." Cindy said typing, "You know not to be that kid but usually when a parent loves a child, breakfast is a thing in the morning."

Kim cut her eyes at her remark. She turned to Rin and frowned.

"If you ever get lonely, get a puppy first."

Rin laughed at them both.

"Cindy, your Mom's had a rough week, we all have really, cut her some slack," she smiled.

Cindy responded to Rin but Kim tuned both their voices out as she was attacked by a sudden sharp migraine. It was small at first but began quickly growing. She cupped her hands on the sides of her head and pressed in hoping to neutralize the pain but it only seemed to get worse and worse. She grunted just quiet enough for neither Cindy nor Rin to notice.

The pain was swelling. She braced herself against the counter and started shaking uncontrollably. She could feel her muscles getting fatigued and her body heating up. She groaned blowing air out from between her lips as the pain grew stronger. She dug her finger nails into the wooden cabinets below the countertop leaving gashes as she pulled back.

She felt like she was erupting from the inside. She had begun sweating, growing short of breath, as the pain grew more and more intense. Then she remembered, eight months ago in the grocery store, on her hands and knees, suffering from an identical experience.

She began to take long deep breaths, calming herself and her nerves. The pain began to slowly fade, she felt her body cooling down, and her strength gradually returned.

She looked back over her shoulder to see Cindy and Rin still talking. They hadn't seemed to notice her suffering mere feet away from them.

She turned her head back around, still attempting to catch her breath. She wiped the sweat from her forehead on her pants leg and looked down at her reflection in the countertop. For once she wasn't entirely disappointed with what she saw. For the first time in what felt like an eternity she saw someone she recognized, herself. Not the person who had a million secrets to keep as she lived the life she thought she had to, but the person who was free and living the life she wanted to. She believed that person had died with her foster parents years ago, but that person was still her, she had just been hidden for some years. She gave herself a small smile.

She looked up from the countertop out the window in front of her and her jaw dropped. Her eyes grew wide and her heart skipped a beat.

Helena stood on the other side motionless,

smiling at her. Her long dark blonde hair was gently flowing in the breeze behind her, shining radiantly from the sun beaming down on it. She looked like a painting come to life as she stood motionless staring at Kim.

Kim broke to her left, running to the front door. Rin and Cindy's heads whipped around at Kim's sudden burst of action. They glanced at each other with puzzled looks before following her over to the door.

Kim yanked the door open, stuck her head out, and looked to the spot Helena had been standing, she wasn't there. She swiveled her head around and looked the other way still unable to find her. She looked towards the bushes, out to the street, down the road, and even up in the trees but couldn't find her.

She took a step out the door and instantly pulled her foot back feeling it land on something soft. She looked down at her doorstep and saw the black beanie Helena always wore resting on her welcome mat.

She picked it up and ran her thumb over the bold white lettering.

"LIVE FREE" it read.

She began to hear an echoing snicker inside her head.

"Too slow K, too slow!"

She recognized her voice immediately. As the snickering eventually faded a heavy sigh followed.

"I think this is it Kim. I think my time is up. I think we're officially one again, and while I don't know what that means for me, I'm excited about what it means for you. Live free Kim, live your life. You got too much of it left to spend worrying about the things you can't change. Be happy, embrace who you are, what you have, you've got a lot more than you might think."

Her voice sounded so big, so powerful, as it rattled inside Kim's head. She got goosebumps as she listened to her speak.

".... but you..." Kim began.

"Awww.... Kim don't worry about me. I'm fine, all I ever wanted was to see my girl happy. Now that I have, whatever happens to me, doesn't matter. It's been real Kim, take care of yourself, keep Rin outta trouble, and tell Cindy, Aunt Helena's gonna miss her."

She sighed heavily again but Kim could tell wherever she was, in whatever form she was in, she was smiling.

"Well, I guess.... I guess this is goodbye," Helena whispered.

A strong wind suddenly burst from the left blowing Kim's hair in front of her eyes. She looked up and saw the trees, bushes, and grass had all fallen victim to the sudden current as well.

As the wind whipped through the air shaking everything in its path Kim came to the conclusion it couldn't have been anything other than her final wave goodbye.

"And oh.... it was the bomb hanging out with you Kim," Helena's voice added in a whisper.

Just as her voice silenced the wind ceased. Kim looked up and down the block in awe. Part of her couldn't believe it but then she remembered who it was. She was long past the point of being surprised by her and anything she did anymore, it was obvious that whatever she was, she was much more than Kim had ever originally imagined her to be.

Memories of their first encounter eight months prior begun to flow back into her mind.

Kim!

Oh my god, I haven't seen you in forever! How are you?

Kim it's me, Helena?

She smiled as she held the knitted beanie in her hands. She ran her thumb over the lettering again. She shook her head smiling as she closed the door. She turned around to Rin and Cindy who were staring at her like she was crazy.

"You good?" Rin asked.

"Yeah.... I'm good," Kim said, smiling at the beanie in her hands.

"What's that?" Rin asked eyeing it.

Kim looked up at her surprised.

"You can see this?" Kim asked.

"What, the hat?" she asked reaching out running her fingers over the lettering, "Yeah? Where'd it come from?"

Kim shrugged shaking her head again.

"A friend of mine," she laughed.

"Oh, OK..." Rin said, still a bit confused.

"Would that friend happen to know how to cook, cause if so, I'm gonna go live with them," Cindy said.

Kim rolled her eyes.

"How bout I start breakfast," Rin laughed, "and you watch and learn, that way you don't have to wait on your Mom anymore."

"Thanks," Kim said to her.

"No problem, you can go get cleaned up. We'll get the food started," she said, gently pushing Cindy back towards the kitchen.

Standing in the front hall Kim listened to the two of them. It tickled her. Her daughter and sister together, enjoying one another's company. It was what she had longed for for years, a family and time to enjoy them.

She looked down at the beanie in her hands and gripped it tight. She began climbing the stairs. She walked into her room and looked around the space. She eventually keyed in on her dresser pressed up against the wall and the tall decorative pillar that rose high over the top of the mirror. She placed the beanie over the pillar with the words facing out. She stepped back to view it and smiled.

A reminder to always live free she thought to herself.

As she looked onto the dresser something fell from inside the beanie. Kim stepped forward and picked up a small piece of scratch paper. On it was a crudely drawn picture of a rabbit done in pen. One of its ears was longer than the other and its eyes were far from evenly shaped. Kim recalled back to the day Helena had first revealed herself as Kim's offset.

Awww.... Kim... I don't even have a phone, I drew a picture of a bunny on that piece of paper.

Her eyes fell to some words written at the

bottom left of the paper and she read, "Love, your offset"

A small heart drawn just to the right of her sign off. Kim couldn't help but smile. She tucked the paper back up inside the beanie.

She walked into her bathroom and leaned over the sink. She again took pleasure in viewing her reflection. Her smile seemed so foreign to her. She couldn't remember the last time she had smiled in a mirror. She turned on the faucet and ran her hands under the cool water. She cupped some in her hands and rubbed it on her face. She dried her face off with a small towel and headed back downstairs.

She stopped as she came to the bottom step and took a seat on it. She peeked through the stair railing into the kitchen and watched.

"You don't wanna use too much, just enough so nothing sticks to the pan OK?" Rin said.

"Mmhmm…" Cindy nodded.

She leaned over and rested her head against the railing as she watched them. With everything she had endured in the past two decades, jumping from home to home, being adopted, reorphaned, living in and out of the streets, joining The Pool, to the fall of The Pool and a few people she held close, to the ultimate loss of those she would've held the closest, Kim had long believed happiness to be unobtainable in her life, but there it stood right in her own kitchen.

She couldn't believe how far things had gone and how much her life had changed in just a matter of days, but she was so happy with where it had ended up.

She closed her eyes and thought about her foster parents, envisioning their faces in her head smiling at her. She recalled the lessons they taught her in humility, respect, and kindness in their time together. The love and care they gave her that bared fruit in the form of ten of the happiest years of her life. She couldn't imagine her life without the chapter of it in which they rescued her and showed her how real happiness could be.

Then to her came an image of her biological parents. Their smiles, their words, as she cried on her knees at their feet.

We missed you darling.

This is…. this is my daughter.

A moment she would never grow tired of reliving, no matter how many times. The stories Rin had shared with her, the stories she promised to one day finish that left her in a state of blissful anticipation. She had so many questions, so many wonders that she couldn't wait to inquire about.

All four of their faces swirled around in her head. She hoped that wherever their souls ended up, that somehow the four of them were able to meet, talk, and share with each other. She hoped all four of them were proud of her. As she had forgiven them, she hoped that they could all forgive her for her mistakes, forgive the sins she turned into work, and above all else, hoped that they knew she loved them all dearly.

But as much hope as she had, as much as she loved them all, she didn't have another moment to spend thinking about things so far out of her control.

She had a long life ahead of her, a life full of moments begging to be made into memories. A wise person had told her to take advantage of her time of freedom, that her happiest days were yet to come. And so, she decided right then and there she was done looking back on her past, remembrance was one thing, but to hopelessly dwell was another.

Still a parent by the minute, and now a loving sister as well. This was her life, her new life, and she already loved it. She decided then from now on she would only look one way, forward. She now had a life to live.

Acknowledgements

I would like to dedicate the following page(s) to thank those that motivated me to keep writing, take a chance on my work, and push for publication. The following individuals were sent or given small excerpts of my work (not necessarily this one) and encouraged me to keep writing whether through their praise or constructive criticism.

Names listed in alphabetical order

Alexis Bright
Aliyah C.
Anna Thompson
Averry Cox
Ayana Reynolds
Brianna Watters
Britney Reynolds
Claire K.
Crane O'Hanlon
David L. Hawks
Erin Elledge
Hannah B. Brennan
Hannah Mokulis
Hephzibah Eniade
Hope Anderson
Izabella N. Vital

Kaliya Williams
Kelsee Piercy
Mackenzie Jolene & the entire Monahan family
Melissa Baez
Nichelle Dew
Nicole Nina Náray
Noor Khalid
Olivia Stephens
Peter Revel-Walsh
Rachel Grace Pigott
Regena Dossett
Romae Jarrett
Star Box
Tyson Hills
Whitney McMahan

I owe a special thanks to Vivien Reis, Jenna Moreci, and Bethany Atazadeh for the tips, advice, and coaching they provided via their Youtube channels. Without you three I could not have become the writer that I am today and the care of which this book was handled from start to finish resulting in the finished product would not be nearly as evident without the many teachings and guidance I received from each of you. Thank you all tremendously.

I owe a huge amount of gratitude to Mrs. Berkleigh Cirilli, one of my beta readers and the teacher who gave me the homework assignment that led to me finding my love for writing. Had it not been for you I probably would have never taken writing seriously and I would have never ended up discovering my love for storytelling. You were the first person to show belief in my writing ability and it means the world to me. Without you, not a word of any short story, novel, or narrative I have ever written would exist. As I have told you many times before I will never forget you, and thank you for everything.

A huge thanks to Zane Alexander for being one of my beta readers and assisting in marketing and exposure of my works. I really appreciate the encouragement and feedback you provided that ultimately let me know my work was good enough to be published. Your creativity and storytelling ability you showcase within your own works inspired me to push myself as I attempted to bring my works to life. And so, I absolutely must thank you for your contributions to this book's existence you may not have even known you made. Thank you Zane.

I must thank Samantha Dambach for all the help and resources she supplied me with to help transition my work from an idea in my head, to a word document on my laptop, to an eventual tangible book. Thank you so much for all the wisdom and knowledge you shared with me on the processes of writing, editing, and publishing. Know this book would not and could not exist today without your help.

To my amazing editor, Michelle Krueger, thank you so so so much. The editing process was something that initially terrified me and though we had some hiccups and slowdowns due to factors far out of either of our control we got through it together and ended up with a fantastic final copy of the book and I cannot thank you enough for that. Your edits, proofing, suggestions, praises, and criticisms were all immensely crucial in the polishing of this book and ultimately me achieving my dream of becoming a published author. Wherever it goes, know "The Joy City Pool" would not and could not be what it is today without you and your contributions to it. Thank you for everything.

Massive amount of thanks to Haze Long for bringing this book's front and back cover art to life. When I first sent you the front cover concept sketch that I did in color pencil I thought the cover would look pretty good but you and your talents made the cover truly great. Then you blew me away again with your incredible execution of the back cover. Looking over the finished product never ceases to amaze me and I'm truly honored to have pieces of your original artwork as my book's cover art. Thank you so much Haze.

Big thanks to Sharon Bailey who narrated the audiobook version of this work. Having the book be widely accessible in many different formats was important to me and so I thank you for lending your talents in helping me accomplish this as well as helping with last bit of polishing/editing of the manuscript.

And of course, I must thank my entire family for the love and support they showed me throughout the entire writing and publishing process.

I can't thank you all enough for the time and effort you sacrificed in contributing to this work. All the things each and every one of you did, told me you loved about my work, or told me you didn't like so much were considered and played a pivotal role in what the final product is today. I hope as you read you were able to take pride in knowing you contributed to this work in one way or another.

Finally, I want to thank any and all who picked up this novel and read it cover to cover. I truly hope you enjoyed your read.

Contact and Social Information

 joycitycontact@gmail.com

 @EverythingJoyCity

 @Everything_JC

 @everythingjoycity

CPSIA information can be obtained
at www.ICGtesting.com
Printed in the USA
BVHW042148051222
653541BV00005B/242